SUCCESSFUL
MARKETING

PAULINE ROWSON

crimson

This edition first published in Great Britain 2009 by
Crimson Publishing, a division of Crimson Business Ltd
Westminster House
Kew Road
Richmond
Surrey
TW9 2ND

A catalogue record for this book is available from the British Library.

ISBN 978 1 85458 481 6

Printed and bound by LegoPrint SpA, Trento

CONTENTS

INTRODUCTION

In order to grow your business, you need to actively market your services or products to your target markets. Even if you are operating in the public sector, or in a non-profit organisation, there is still the need to communicate successfully with your customers and potential customers.

But how do you get customers? How do you get them to buy from you – and not just once but again and again? How do you build a competitive edge for your business? How do you develop new products and services and stay ahead of the competition? And how do you communicate the right message in the right way? All these and many more are the challenges for a business, and they are questions that will be answered in this book.

I will show you in a straightforward, practical style how to use a variety of marketing techniques, to win more business. There are lots of tips throughout the book and a handy summary of the points covered at the end of each chapter for easy reference.

This guide will show you:
- How to identify and target your customers and potential customers
- How to develop and build a competitive edge
- How to write a marketing plan
- How to use the various promotional tools more successfully
- How to integrate email marketing and the Internet into your marketing strategy.

Author's note: To avoid confusion and the cumbersome use of 'he' and 'she', 'he' has been adopted throughout this guide. No prejudice is intended.

PART 1

INTRODUCTION TO MARKETING

CHAPTER 1

What is successful marketing?

All businesses have one thing in common: they need customers. Without customers quite simply there is no business. Rather obvious, you might be thinking, but it's amazing how many people forget this time and time again. This chapter examines what is meant by marketing and how to adopt a marketing philosophy for your organisation.

Successful marketing is:

- About knowing your customers and communicating with them in the most effective way in order to win more business from them. It is about understanding who your customers are and anticipating what they want, not just today or tomorrow, but next year, the year after, and so on.
- Having a business that is flexible enough to respond quickly to changing demands. And a workforce that is willing to cooperate with your customers, not treat them as if they were public enemy number one.
- Not something that you can pick up today and get results from tomorrow. It is not an ad hoc activity to be actioned when the mood takes you. Neither is it simply placing an advertisement and then waiting for the telephone to ring and orders to flood in, because it just doesn't happen that way.

Successful marketing is about relaying a consistent message to your customers and your target customers in a way that they can understand.

There is no great mystery to successful marketing. Much of it is applying basic common sense with an added touch of creativity. And before you get worried about that word 'creativity', let me define it by saying all you need is the ability to open your mind and to put yourself in your customers' shoes.

Successful marketing means putting the customer at the heart of your business so that everything you do is driven by that philosophy. The definition of what marketing means from the **Chartered Institute of Marketing** summarises all the above points very well.

'Marketing is the management process responsible for identifying, anticipating and satisfying customer requirements profitably.'
Chartered Institute of Marketing

This might sound like a tall order, but if you take a planned approach to your marketing, it isn't. I am going to show you how to do this. So let's start by seeing just how marketing-friendly your organisation is. Take a look at the questions below and see how your organisation rates.

ACTION POINT

How marketing orientated is your business? Can you tick yes to all of these questions?

☐ Are your services or products created with the customer in mind?

☐ Do you track your customers' attitudes and behaviour?

☐ Is your business organised and coordinated in the service of your customers?

☐ Are you and your staff customer-friendly and responsive to your customers' needs?

☐ Are your staff motivated and all pulling in the same direction?

☐ Does the same vision and identity exist both inside and outside the organisation?

☐ Do you consistently deliver your promises?

☐ Are you in business to make a profit?

☐ Do you innovate enough?

So how did you score? Were you able to tick all the boxes? If so, well done, but it is not enough to be able to tick them once – today. If you wish to build and maintain your competitive edge then you have to keep asking these questions and keep ticking the boxes – everyday!

If you were to give this list to a customer would he tick 'yes' to all the boxes?

Let's look at these points more closely.

CUSTOMER FOCUSED PRODUCTS

Are you producing what your customers want, and not what you *think* they want or what you like producing? You might be very good at making widgets, but it's not a bit of good if no one wants to buy them.

The question is not as simple as it first appears because customers' needs and wants change, technology advances and fashion alters. Companies can spend thousands of pounds researching and developing products only to find that they are too late to introduce them into the marketplace and that demand has either been met by someone else or the fashion has changed and the product has been superseded.

Alternatively, the product or service you have developed could be ahead of its time and therefore result in poor take-up. Timing is often a very difficult element to judge. The only way to find out if your products or services are what your customers want is to ask them for feedback – and even more importantly, listen to what they say.

TOP TIPS

You need to monitor your market and your competitors, to talk and listen to your staff, to look at what is happening in the wider marketplace and be aware of trends and developments, which could affect your business.

Your customers' attitudes and behaviour

You need to be constantly in touch with your customers. How often do you talk to them? How often do you survey them? Do you know what your customers buy, how they buy and when they buy? Do you know what they want from you?

CUSTOMER FOCUSED BUSINESS

Not only do you have to give the customers what they want, but you also have to deliver the product or service in the way they want. For example, if your customers wish to be invoiced monthly, then invoice them monthly. If they wish to buy online then make sure you provide them with this service. Or perhaps they want free delivery. Are you able to provide this? Listen to your customers and constantly review your business practices. Is your business structured in the correct way to meet demand? Do you have the right level and type of staff to deal efficiently with customer needs? This brings me on to my next point.

FRIENDLY AND RESPONSIVE STAFF

Have you ever heard any of your staff say the following?
- 'We've being doing it this way for the last 20 years' (which, of course, means they can't possibly change).
- 'Well you must appreciate that we have our administration to think about.'
- 'It's more costly for us to do it that way.'
- No-one else has ever complained about doing it this way.'
- That's just our policy.'

And so on and so on…excuses, excuses…

Perhaps you are too busy to stop and think about the way you are doing things – but if you don't make time to do this, then you could be missing out on valuable opportunities. Finding new ways of supplying and servicing your customers is what will give you a competitive edge. What was acceptable 10, five or even a year ago might not be acceptable today and will certainly change tomorrow. Make sure you employ the right staff for the right jobs.

Q EXAMPLE

A busy theatre employed telephone handling staff to take bookings over the telephone. Many customers who phoned in would ask questions about the show before deciding whether or not to purchase tickets. Questions such as: was the show any good? Where were the best seats? Which nights were the best to attend? Will I enjoy the performance? Is it my type of show? Some of these questions were quite simple to answer but others required tactful handling and were a matter of personal taste.

The telephone operator might not like the show that was being performed but he would need to provide the customer with an impartial answer, perhaps by quoting reviews the show had received. He would need to treat each caller as an individual, no matter how many times that day he had been asked the same questions. Handling these calls requires someone with excellent communication skills, patience and the ability to steer the caller into buying tickets for the show as quickly as possible to free up the lines for waiting callers; not someone who treats the customer as a fool and ditherer, or someone who bullies the customer into making too rapid a decision that they feel uncomfortable with it.

MOTIVATED STAFF

Do you know where your business is heading? I hope so, but have you communicated that to your staff? If they don't know then how can you expect them to help you achieve your aims? You need your staff working for you and not against you.

CONSISTENT VISION AND IDENTITY

Do you know what your organisation stands for in the marketplace? If you don't, how do you expect your staff to deliver it?

ACTION POINT

1. Write down at least three keywords that you believe describes your business.
2. Get your staff together, or in small groups if you have lots of staff, and ask them to write down on a piece of paper three words which they believe describes the business.
3. Put all these words up on a flip chart or white board. Did you all come up with the same words or do the staff see the business differently from you?
4. Now repeat the exercise asking some of your customers. Is this a million miles from how you see your organisation? If so what do you need to change to marry the two together?

Here are some words that might be used to describe an organisation's personality:
- Professional
- Friendly
- Helpful
- Hi-tech
- Efficient

Once you have defined the personality of your company, ask yourself if this personality is communicated both within the company and outside it. Is the same message being communicated? If not, then conflict and confusion will arise and you will be wasting effort, not to mention money, and you will lose potential business.

DELIVERY OF YOUR PROMISES

Organisations that consistently deliver what they promise will gain a competitive advantage. Unfortunately many businesses fail to deliver time after time. Sometimes this is caused by over-promising and sometimes by gross inefficiencies. If this is happening in your organisation then all the money you spend trying to win new business (your sales and marketing budget) might just as well be poured down the drain. There is no point working hard to win customers if you lose them through failing to deliver what they want.

MAKING A PROFIT

Are you in business to make a profit? The answer to this is fairly obvious. Yes. And even non-profit-making organisations have to balance budgets and make them stretch ever further these days. Charities need revenue and to make every donation count, and schools need to make their budgets stretch to almost impossible lengths. So you need to make every penny you spend on your marketing count.

IMPORTANCE OF INNOVATION

How often do you look at producing new services or products for your customers or examine new ways of doing things? The organisation which innovates is the one that is going to build and maintain a competitive edge.

 **ACTION POINT**

1. Make a list of the services or products your company produces – are these what the customer wants?
2. Conduct a survey with your customers. Telephone a sample of customers, or devise a questionnaire to capture their comments after a transaction.
3. Gain feedback from your staff if they regularly interface with your customers. What are your customers telling your staff?
4. Listen and act upon this, even if you don't like what you are hearing!

QUICK RECAP

- *Marketing is a long-term strategy not a short-term one.*
- *Marketing is a management philosophy that should run right through your business.*
- *Marketing means getting to know your customers and thinking like them.*
- *Marketing is giving your customers what they want, when they want it, how they want it and delivering it in a profitable way.*
- *Marketing is anticipating what your customers will want in the future and ensuring you deliver this.*
- *Marketing is about creating your services/products with the customer in mind.*
- *Marketing is making sure your staff are motivated and all pulling in the same direction.*
- *Marketing is about consistently delivering your promises and innovating to gain a competitive edge.*

CHAPTER 2

Know your customers

The key to effective marketing is knowing your customers, understanding their needs and desires and communicating with them in an effective manner. Without this knowledge, the marketing you undertake could be guess work and therefore a waste of time, money and energy. This chapter looks at understanding who your customers are and how to segment them into clearly identifiable groups, thereby making it far more cost effective and easier to target them.

First let me start by asking you **seven key marketing questions**.

1. What business are you in?

This is not as straightforward as it seems. For example, if you are a book publisher then you might assume your business is printing and selling books – but it isn't. Depending upon the types of book a publisher produces he can be in the business of entertaining, educating, informing, providing escapism or all four.

2. Who buys my products or services?

To continue with our publishing example, students and academics will buy educational textbooks; managers, directors, self-employed people and students will buy business books. But many diverse groups of people from different socioeconomic and ethnic backgrounds, and of varying age groups, will buy fiction novels.

Your organisation might have a wide range of services or products and therefore many different groups of customers. This means that a one-size-fits-all solution will not succeed.

In order to successfully market to your customers, you need to fully understand who they are.

3. What do I know about my target markets?

What is your customers' lifestyle? What do they enjoy doing in their spare time? How do they spend their money? Where do they shop, what are their beliefs, their age, ethnic backgrounds?

If you are marketing business-to-business, what do you know about the industry sector you are targeting? What are the buying patterns? Who is the decision maker? Why would they buy your products?

4. What do your customers want?

Do you understand your customers' needs, their problems, desires and tastes?

5. Where are your customers?

Where do they live? Which area or country?

6. How do you reach them?

What do they read, listen to, or watch on television? Are they internet or technologically savvy? Do they attend conferences or exhibitions?

7. What messages will they respond to?

What sort of images and language would they respond to? How can you persuade them to buy? How can you inform or educate them?

If you have answered all the questions satisfactorily then well done, but you might like to review your answers after reading this book to see if you are on the right track, or if you can improve your marketing further by being more specific in your answers. I will return to many of these questions throughout this book.

First though, having a clear understanding of your target market is essential to effective marketing.

> The more you know about your customers the easier it will be for you to choose and use the appropriate marketing tool and message to reach them.

This isn't always easy. Your customers may be a different age or gender to you. They may have a very different lifestyle. They may come from very different backgrounds or from across a number of diverse industries. They may come from around the globe. But whoever they are, and wherever they are, it is your task to understand them and then to communicate with them. You need to suspend your own beliefs and values and think like your target customers.

UNDERSTANDING YOUR CUSTOMERS

In order to understand your customers it is easier if you divide them into identifiable groups with similar characteristics. This way you can also target them more effectively. By understanding and targeting the right group, you can sell more to *them* and stop throwing away money chasing customers who are unlikely to buy from you.

DIVIDING CUSTOMERS INTO GROUPS

If you are already running a business, or you are a manager or executive in a non-profit organisation, the best place to start is by analysing your existing customer base to establish what type of people or businesses currently buy from you. If you are starting a new business, you need to have a clear idea of your future potential markets and you can do this by following the guidelines below.

Begin by dividing your customers into two distinct groups: business and consumers. Some organisations will be operating in both markets, others only in the one. From these two groups you can then subdivide your customers further.

Business markets

Type of business
Pinpoint what business sectors your customers are in. Are they in the construction industry, computing, engineering, retail, etc? You may have customers in a diverse range of industries. Give each industry sector a code on your database; you can then analyse these customer sectors to see what they are buying from you, how much and when. You will also be able to target them more effectively because different sectors speak different business languages, they require different products and services from you, and even if they all buy the same product/service, their needs will vary.

Different companies will have different needs; they will speak different business languages.

Size of business
Are your customers from large, medium or small companies? Or are they from a range of these? There are many ways you can define size: by turnover, the number of outlets or branches, or the number of employees.

By geographical area
Where are your customers based? Are they local, national or worldwide? What is the best way of reaching them? Is it by telephone, a personal visit, letter, email, the internet or at exhibitions etc? How will this affect your marketing and pricing?

Q EXAMPLE

James runs a printing company which provides a range of services from long-run litho printing (glossy brochures, leaflets) to personalised short-run digital printing (leaflets, personalised newsletters, flyers, brochures, stationery). He has always considered that any business can buy his printing services so he has spent (and wasted) a great deal of money on advertising in directories, at football grounds, in newspapers and business magazines. His advertising campaign has brought him no new business, now he wonders what he has done wrong.

While it's true that any business could buy from James, this is far too wide a definition, and therefore too broad a market for him to reach. He wasted money by not understanding who his core customers are. James needs to identify who his target customers are for both his litho printing division and his personalised digital printing services. Then having identified them he can target his marketing to reach them. He – and you – can do this by following the exercise below.

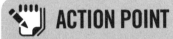 **ACTION POINT**

To work out your target markets, start by analysing your current customer base.
• Make a list of your key customers.
• Against their names, list their business sector and their size.
• Are they small, medium or large companies?
• Are they from the public sector?

Now list what services or products they buy.
• How often do they buy?
• Where are they based?
• Is there a pattern emerging?

Which of your customers are your most profitable sectors?
You might be able to categorise them further into top, middle or lower-tiered customers, or label your list category A for top and highly profitable customers; B for those who are good customers but not so profitable, and C for customers who give you work regularly and who are good referrers of business. Now ask the question: can I target my marketing to reach more of these types of customer? The answer has to be yes. Keep this list beside you as you go through the rest of this book and afterwards when you put together your marketing plan.

Consumer markets

The area of consumer marketing is very sophisticated and some companies spend vast amounts of money in understanding just exactly who their customers are. Information on the breakdown of the population is provided through the government-led census. This information is taken by companies and agencies and cross referenced with other information gathered through surveys, research etc to provide organisations with a breakdown of consumers: their buying habits, where they live, their occupation, leisure interests, age, social status and so on. The loyalty cards issued by many large stores are just another means of capturing information about the buying habits and breakdown of customers. And the internet can provide organisations with information on the buying patterns of their customers or their preferences by analysing the web pages they view, how often, when and where the customer comes from.

Your own database is the best place to start in analysing your customers. Start by capturing information about your customers, even if this is only their address to begin with. If you have postal codes then you can use a research agency to help analyse where your customers come from and their lifestyles and backgrounds. It is frightening how much information there is on each individual out there. Bear in mind you will have to pay for services of a research agency. However, common sense can also help you analyse your customer base, as most businesses will have some idea about their customers. So if you are in consumer markets then you can divide your customers by the following categories.

By type of house

Are your target customers more likely to live in a large, detached modern house or a terraced house in an inner city? Do they live in council houses or in cottages in the country? Do they rent or own their property? And what area of the country do they live in? Is it town, suburb, countryside or do your customers come from a mixture of these?

By lifestyle

What is their lifestyle? What hobbies do they enjoy? Do they go out to eat, and if so where? Where do they shop and what sort of goods do they buy? Do they take holidays abroad and if so what kind of holiday? What newspapers and magazines do they read?

By lifecycle

Are they married or single? Do they live together? Do they have children, and if so what are the ages of the children. This will influence what is bought. Are they retired and if so how affluent?

You can also divide your customers by:

- Age
- Gender
- Ethnic origin
- Marital status
- Employment status
- Income

🔍 EXAMPLE

The Wellton Hotel is a four-star modern hotel situated just off a motorway and close to a major city. It has easy access from road and rail networks and ample parking. It also has a wide range of facilities including conference rooms, a gym, swimming pool, golf course and leisure centre. Its target markets are both consumers and businesses.

Being a four-star hotel it is more expensive than the average hotel so its marketing campaigns are targeted at: those with a higher disposable income; those who belong to a fitness and/ or leisure club; those who regularly travel by road or rail; those whose occupations involve travelling, such as sales managers/ directors or business owners/managers; those businesses who hire conference rooms for product launches or seminars and training.

ACTION POINT

If you are in consumer markets, list your key customers.

Make notes on their lifestyle, their lifecycle, ages and hobbies.

- What magazines/newspapers would they read?
- What are their spending habits?
- Where are they based?

Keep this list/information by you as you read the rest of this book and certainly when you come to plan your marketing.

BUT WHAT IF I CAN SELL TO EVERYBODY?

Some business owners have told me that 'anybody' can buy their products/services, and of course that is possible. If someone turns up at the hotel wanting to stay overnight, the hotel isn't going to turn business away – but that is very different from 'targeting' customers.

You can **sell** your products/services to whoever is prepared to pay for them, but when it comes to **marketing**, it is almost impossible to market to 'anybody' unless you have a great deal of money to throw away. Besides, what message do you use? It would have to appeal to a very wide range of people with diverse interests and backgrounds – that means that sometimes your marketing message will hit the right note with the right people; the rest of the time it will be wasted and so will your money.

You need to make your marketing work, so don't waste time and money chasing customers who are unlikely to buy from you, or who are unprofitable. Know what markets you are in and understand those markets thoroughly. It will pay dividends.

> By analysing your customer groups clearly you can begin to answer the questions:
> - Where are my customers?
> - How do I reach them?
> - How do I communicate with them?

When you look at your target groups of customers you will probably find that some groups are easier to reach than others. Some will be more profitable or better payers. It is these you want to concentrate on.

Once having decided *who* to target, you can then decide *how* to target them. Where can you advertise? What other promotional tools would they respond to? In addition, what sort of message would appeal to them and what kind of image? We'll cover more of this in later chapters, but if you don't undertake this first basic exercise then you could be advertising, or sending your mailshots and e-shots to the wrong people – a waste of time and money.

TOP TIPS

Once you have defined your customer segments you need to ask the following questions:

■ How large is that group of customers?

■ Where are they and how easy is it for me to reach them?

■ How many competitors are in the marketplace in relation to that group?

■ How can what I am offering be significantly different to my competitors?

■ How easy is it to enter or win new business from this group?

The answers to the above questions will help you decide where you should be spending both your money and time on marketing. You might also need to adopt different marketing tactics for different groups of customers.

YOUR EXISITING CUSTOMERS

Above all don't forget to continue marketing to your existing customers. Could you be selling more to them? Your existing customers are the easiest group of people to sell to, yet many businesses overlook them and keep chasing the Holy Grail of new business.

Once you have analysed your customer base to see which ones are giving you the most business, and which have the potential to give you a high volume and value of business, focus your marketing activities on these, your core customers. For most businesses, 80% of business comes from 20% of customers, therefore look at ways to keep these customers loyal. Ensure that your products or services are genuinely delivering what these customers want.

Be flexible and respond to your customers' needs quickly. Keep your name in front of your customers so they don't forget you are around – this is particularly important in a recession. Those businesses that continue with their marketing during a recession not only win the limited amount of business available but are in a far stronger position when the good times return.

TOP TIPS

■ Look at your own customer base and analyse who is buying from you.
■ Start capturing information about your customers on a database and analyse it on a regular basis.

Don't forget dormant or past customers. Find out why they stopped buying from you and try to win them back.

QUICK RECAP

- *Identify who your customers are. Break your customers down into easily identifiable groups with similar characteristics.*
- *Examine what each group of customers buy, how much and when.*
- *Look at the groups of customers in relation to your marketplace.*
- *Keep in regular touch with your existing customers; try to up-sell and cross-sell other products and services to them.*
- *Find out why customers have stopped buying from you and try to win them back.*

CHAPTER 3

Know what your customers are buying and why

Having looked at who your customers are, you now need to understand what they buy and why they buy. This chapter examines how customers buy the benefits of a product or service and the objective and subjective reasons that form their buying decisions. It also looks at the difference between organisational and consumer buying and the marketplace.

Understanding exactly what your customers are buying will help you target them with the right message. When people buy, they ask, 'Why should I? What's in it for me?'. They are seeking certain benefits from buying a particular product or service. It is these benefits that you need to communicate strongly in your advertising and promotional campaigns in order to persuade your customers to buy from you. You also need to communicate these benefits in a creative, stimulating, informative and interesting way. So let's look at features and benefits in more detail.

FEATURES AND BENEFITS

People buy the benefits of a product or service not the features.

Here is a simple example to show you what I mean:

Q EXAMPLE

Anchor Limited is a chandlery based on the south coast of England, offering a wide range of goods to the marine industry. Tim, their sales director, has been asked to draw up a list of the company's features and benefits.

Feature		Benefit
Anchor Limited offer for sale a wide range of marine-related products and equipment	Which means	We have everything under one roof for the customer, saving him time and hassle
Anchor Limited also has a comprehensive website offering online buying 24/7	Which means	It is simple and quick for the customer to buy at a time when it suits him

Anchor Limited has easy access from main roads and is situated close to a major marina with free parking	Which means	There are no parking problems, and the company is easy to reach, saving the customer time, money and hassle
Anchor Limited has been established for 10 years	Which means	The customer can trust us. We are reliable and experienced, with a good reputation and have many satisfied customers, so there are no nasty surprises.
Anchor Limited also offers free delivery to your door or to your boat within a 25-mile radius	Which means	It is convenient and easy to buy from us, and our free delivery saves the customer time and money

The two magic words that turn a feature into a benefit are *which means*.

Below is another example and here I have taken this exercise one stage further:

Q EXAMPLE

I have a laptop computer and I need to convince you that you should also buy one. By stressing the benefits, I am likely to be far more successful.

- *It is lightweight, which means it isn't heavy to carry and therefore won't pull your arms out of their sockets.*
- *It is highly portable, which means you can continue working wherever you are – in the airport, on the train, in someone else's office or at home, therefore helping you to meet tight deadlines.*
- *It is Wi-Fi enabled, which means you can access the internet and pick up your emails wherever you are, enabling you to stay in touch with important clients.*

With the example above I have not only stressed the benefits but have also strengthened them. For example: 'It is Wi-Fi enabled, **which means** you can access the internet and pickup your emails wherever you are (*that's the benefit*) **enabling** you to stay in touch with important clients (*strengthening the benefit*).' You will see I have also done this in the Anchor Limited examples but in case you missed it, here is one of the features and benefits again:

Anchor Limited also offers free delivery to your door or to your boat within a 25-mile radius	**Which means**	It is convenient and easy to buy from us (*the benefit*), and our free delivery saves the customer time and money (*strengthening the benefit*)

So in essence you could draw up four columns rather than three.

Divide a piece of paper into four columns. Head up the columns: **Feature, Which means, Benefit, Therefore**

- Take one of your products or services and now list the features
- Then using the words 'which means' in the second column, translate what that benefit means to your customers and add it to the third column
- Now go one step further and add in the strengthening benefit in the fourth column.

For example:

Feature	**Which means**	**Benefit**	**Therefore**
This marketing book is written in a straightforward, practical style	Which means	It is easy to read and understand	Helping you to be more successful with your marketing and to grow your business.

If you are uncertain of the benefits your customers are buying when they purchase goods or services from your organisation then simply ask them. You can then use some of their comments in your advertising and promotional literature.

So far so good, but it's not just about communicating features and benefits: it's also about conveying the right atmosphere or image around the product or service. So we also need to look at **why people buy.**

People generally buy for two reasons: objective and subjective.

Individuals will buy some products or services to satisfy a basic **physiological need**, ie to satisfy hunger and thirst, to be free from pain or injury, for security or safety reasons, or because they have to comply with the law. These are the **objective reasons** why people buy.

However, it is not always simply a question of needing or wanting a product or service to serve a specific purpose, or to satisfy that basic physiological need that stimulates an individual to buy.

Q EXAMPLE

There are many headache tablets on the market that can banish pain, but how do you get the consumer to buy your headache pill? How do make it stand out from the competition?

*The feature of your headache pill might be some kind of unique formula; the benefit of this means that the customer's headache will vanish within an instant! But the customer will also be asking other questions about the product before deciding to buy and these will be the **subjective reasons**.*

The customer might be influenced by the trade name, which communicates reliability and reputation. Or the product might be endorsed by a highly respected and well-known medical organisation or doctor. Perhaps the colour of the packaging or the design of the product look reassuring and attracts the customer. Or maybe the product is the most expensive on the market and our customer only wants to be seen to be buying 'the best' for himself or his loved ones. These are the subjective reasons.

> The subjective reasons are personally based and are referred to as the psychological reasons involved in buying.

The **subjective or psychological reasons for buying a product or a service** can be summed up as follows:

- To give pleasure
- To give a sense of satisfaction
- To feed and raise self esteem
- To satisfy and feed an ego
- To reinforce group identity and to give a sense of belonging
- To satisfy the need for power
- To satisfy the need for recognition
- To satisfy the need for approval
- To satisfy the need for respect.

These are some of the aspects that you need to take into consideration when communicating your advertising message.

Buying a service

A service is intangible. It cannot be seen, touched or tasted like a product. People deliver services and therefore the maxim 'people buy people' is even more relevant and vital here.

So, when people buy a legal service for example, the **objective reasons** are that they need a lawyer to help them resolve a problem. The **subjective reasons** are:

- Does this lawyer have an understanding of my situation?
- Does he have the technical expertise to deal with my problem?
- Will I understand what he is telling me?
- Will I be able to contact him when I need to?
- Does this lawyer and law firm have a good reputation?
- Are the staff friendly and helpful?
- Is the lawyer efficient?
- Is the chemistry right between the lawyer and me? Do we get on?

- Can he deal with all my legal matters and therefore save me time?
- Does the lawyer come recommended by my peers?

The advertising messages here then must not only communicate features and benefits but also convey some or all of the above.

CONSUMER BUYING VS. BUSINESS BUYING

The obvious difference between consumer and business buying is that consumers buy for their own personal use whilst businesses buy for their organisations.

Generally speaking in a business there are more people involved in the buying decision. You could find that the person who uses the equipment, as well as the person who places the order and the person who authorises the purchase could all influence the buying decision.

Organisations can also impose buying policies and the purchasing decision usually generates lots of paperwork. Decisions will be made on what that organisation needs as opposed to what it wants.

The need to buy in an organisation can take into account the objectives of the company, the policies and procedures. The profit motive may be a strong factor in reaching a purchasing decision. However, not all decisions to buy are based on these objective reasons but often subjective reasons come into play, for example the decision to purchase may also be made based on the relationship you have with the decision maker and whether or not he likes you.

In some organisations there are professional buyers. These are expert in analysing the needs of the company and whether or not the product or service bought match these needs.

Reciprocal buying arrangements may also mean that firms buy from firms that buy from them and supplier loyalty may be involved.

A greater flexibility is often needed in financial arrangements. This could involve options to lease, rent, or give an extension of credit or provide buy-back arrangements.

Many industrial products are expensive to develop and manufacture, as well as being expensive to purchase, so it could mean that the buying cycle is longer. Industrial buyers of capital equipment may take a few years to make a decision to buy from you and this can be the same in professional markets where the decision to change accountants or lawyers could take many years.

Many organisations will seek tenders by buyers for goods and services, and contracts may be drawn up for long-term supply arrangements rather than for one-off purchases.

The buying process in a large company will be very different from a small company. Although the order value may be higher in a large company it could take you longer to sell your products or services because you may have to go through several people until you reach the decision maker, whereas in a smaller business you will normally reach the decision maker a great deal quicker.

THE MARKETPLACE

So you know who your customers are, and you know your products and services, but your business doesn't operate in isolation. You will have competitors. Charities will be competing against each other for donations, volunteers and supporters; public sector can be competing against the private sector; schools against schools for pupils, staff and resources; and businesses for their share of the market.

You will need to have some idea of the size of your market, of who is operating in it and what they are providing. In addition, you will need to have some idea of where you are positioned in relation to them.

✊ ACTION POINT

- List five of your competitors in one of your main product or service areas.
- Now against each one list their strengths and then their weaknesses.
- Where are you positioned in relation to them?
- What makes you better than or different from your competitors?

It isn't always easy to answer these questions as the market-place continually changes. You might have many different competitors for each of your products or services. New competitors will enter your market and your customers' requirements will change. You need to keep abreast of this and adapt your products or services, or the way they are delivered, to suit changing expectations.

Monitoring the competition

So how do you find out who your competitors are? And how do you monitor their activity?

Take time to read your trade magazines and both the local and national newspapers. Not only will they provide you with information about what is happening in your marketplace and the wider market but also about your competitor activity. What are your competitors doing? Are they launching new products, running special offers or recruiting staff? Are they expanding or contracting? Make sure you look at your main competitors' websites from time to time. Do they have a regular e-zine or newsletter? Can you get someone outside your company to subscribe to this?

You might also be able to get information on your comp-etitors' activity from the following:

- Government organisations such as the Chambers of Commerce
- Government Statistical Services

- Trade associations, institutes etc
- Company searches on your competitors

Networking

Ensure that you, or someone in your organisation, get out and about. Attend exhibitions, seminars, business lunches. If you employ a sales force then make sure they give you feedback on what your competitors are doing because they will get information from your customers.

Many times a business owner has said quite confidently to me that they have no competitors and that they are operating in a niche market. Be warned: if what you are providing is good, someone at some stage will jump in and steal your thunder. Also be careful that you don't spend so much time gazing at your competitor's navel that you take your eye from what is happening in your own organisation.

TOP
TIPS

- ■ Take time to read your trade magazines and both the local and national newspapers.
- ■ Review your main competitors' websites from time to time.
- ■ Get someone outside your company to subscribe to a competitors e-zine or newsletter.
- ■ Network – get out and about.
- ■ Attend exhibitions, seminars, business lunches.
- ■ Get feedback from your sales force if you have one.

QUICK RECAP

- *Understanding exactly what your customers are buying will help you send the right message to them.*
- *When people buy they ask themselves the question, 'What's in it for me?'*
- *You need to communicate the benefits of your products or services in your advertising and promotional campaigns.*
- *The two magic words that turn a feature into a benefit are* which means.
- *People generally buy for two reasons: objective and subjective.*
- *Individuals will buy some products or services to satisfy this basic **physiological needs**. These are the **objective reasons** why people buy.*
- *The subjective reasons are personally based and are referred to as the **psychological reasons** involved in buying.*
- *Know your marketplace and your competitors.*

CHAPTER 4

Developing products and services that sell

Organisations need to be constantly looking at providing better, newer, different and more profitable products, or examining better ways of delivering services to customers. Nothing stays the same. Not in life, and certainly not in the business world. The demand for your products or services will change over a period of time. The challenge is to make sure you monitor that change and keep adapting or developing new products and services to meet your customers' changing needs. This chapter explores how you do that through the concept of the **product lifecycle**.

> The product lifecycle states that products go through certain phases: introduction, growth, maturity and decline.

Most companies have a range of products or services each of which may be in a different stage of its lifecycle: introduction, growth, maturity and decline. However, not all products follow this lifecycle. Indeed, some have been around for a very long time and have not gone into decline:

Q EXAMPLE

The Marmite Food Company was established in 1902 and later became Marmite Limited. Marmite was added in soldiers' ration packs in the First World War and became a staple dietary supplement in prisoner-of-war camps in the Second World War. It was also given to the soldiers in Kosovo in 1999. Marmite has expanded its customer base from Great Britain and is now available in 25 countries worldwide.

Other products which haven't declined include Mars bars, and Coca Cola. Conversely, some products never reach the growth phase but fail on introduction.

Q EXAMPLE

The Sinclair C5 was a revolutionary electric vehicle weighing in at 99lb and created by the innovator and inventor Sir Clive Sinclair, most famous for his ZX80 and ZX81 personal computers in 1980s. The C5 was launched on 10 January 1985 in poor weather. This, and the fact that its design was very low and therefore it could not be seen by other vehicles, caused it to receive hostile media coverage from day one. The Sinclair C5 was a commercial disaster. Only around 12,000 C5s were ever produced, many sold off abroad after the project folded. It is, however, today much sought after by collectors.

And then, of course, there is the stage before introduction – **product development**. Many products will never see the introduction phase; whilst others will go on to become mature products.

TOP TIPS

The key to successful growth lies in a company having a number of products or services at the different stages of its lifecycle. This will also determine your marketing strategy, investment costs and profitability.

Let's take a look at this in more detail.

Product development
* There is no return on your investment
* You have a heavy investment both in terms of time and money.

Introduction (the beginning of the product lifecycle)
• Your sales are low
• Your cash flow is negative
• Your profits are negligible
• You are searching out new customers
• Your investment costs are high/marketing costs high.

Growth
• Your sales are growing fast
• Your profits are at peak levels
• Your customers are growing
• Your marketing costs are moderate to high.

Maturity
• Your sales are starting to slow before going into decline
• Your profits are declining
• Your marketing costs could be high as you struggle to keep your products in front of your customers to boost sales.

Decline
- Your sales are declining
- Your profits are declining
- Your cash flow levels are low
- Customers are fewer.

When a product or service is in the growth phase, its sales will be high and investment costs lower. Profit should then be reinvested into new product or service development so that when a product reaches maturity and declines there are other products and services coming along behind it to stimulate sales.

 **ACTION POINT**

- Look at your products and services.
- Identify which products are at what stage in the product lifecycle.

EXTENDING THE LIFECYCLE

You can extend the product lifecycle and halt decline by **adapting your product or service**. This means taking an existing product or service and adapting it for an existing market, or selling it into a completely new market.

Adapting can include:
- Modifying or improving the product itself
- Improving or changing the quality
- Changing the packaging
- Changing the name
- Relaunching it
- Targeting a completely new market or new geographical area, or even country
- Offering a sales incentive to buy.

Mars has extended their product's lifecycle by reintroducing the Mars bar in a number of different forms. There has been king size, party pack size, miniature size, egg shaped, filled with ice cream and dark chocolate.

Marmite however has not done a great deal to extend its product lifecycle by adapting the product; instead it has found new markets by expanding into other countries. The company started using glass jars in the 1920s. The shape of the jar and the distinctive red and yellow label have remained pretty much the same since then. However, the company has introduced a 'Squeeze Me' version, and its website ably demonstrates how it has extended the product lifecycle by showing how Marmite can be used in a variety of different recipes with celebrity chef endorsement and a clever 'love it or hate it' advertising campaign. Sales of Marmite continue to grow.

If sales of one of your product or service are declining you need to examine the following options:

• Ditch it immediately
• See if you can extend its lifecycle by a rapid makeover and re-launch
• Increase the price dramatically before ditching it and get some revenue
• Sell the product or service on
• Adopt certain sales promotion tactics, eg offering 10% off or 10% extra.

Be warned though that trying to extend the product's lifecycle by adopting certain sales promotions techniques such as special offers and discounts will have an impact on your profitability.

ACTION POINT

• Taking your list of products and services created earlier, identify those products or services in decline.
• State what action you will take: ditch or extend.
• State how you think you can extend the product or service.

Product differentiation has become a key competitive strategy and new product development an essential activity.

Here is another way of looking at your product or service development. This is called **The Boston Consulting Group Model** and it relates market and company variables to performance, with the basis of performance being measured in cash flow.

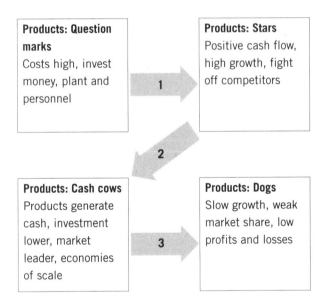

| Products: Question marks
Costs high, invest money, plant and personnel | 1 → | Products: Stars
Positive cash flow, high growth, fight off competitors |
| Products: Cash cows
Products generate cash, investment lower, market leader, economies of scale | 3 → | Products: Dogs
Slow growth, weak market share, low profits and losses |

The Boston Consulting Group Model

- Careful and continuous watch must be kept on competitors when your products are in the star phase, lest any of them gain leadership in market share and therefore threaten your cash flow.
- It is vital to achieve a good balance in terms of financial and managerial resources among cash cows, question marks and star businesses.
- In time question marks will become stars – or dogs. Stars will become cows, or if inadequately nourished – dogs!

DEVELOPING NEW PRODUCTS/SERVICES

You will need to be on the constant lookout for new products or services. So where can you get ideas from?

Listening to your staff

Your staff may have a wealth of ideas but they need to be encouraged to air them. You need to create a climate where ideas can be raised and welcomed, not shot down in flames. New staff in particular should be encouraged to come forward with ideas and suggestions on how to improve things because they come into the organisation with fresh eyes.

Your staff may also have more contact with the customer than you. You need to encourage your staff to ask the customers questions about the level of satisfaction experienced with the product or service. Staff should then feed these comments back to you. Of course, it goes without saying that you should take those comments onboard and take action if possible.

Listening to your customers

You can carry out formal research amongst your customers, asking them for their views and opinions. Or the research can be informal. Simply by asking customers what they think about your products or services can be enough. Don't forget to listen to their comments and act on them. Customer evaluation forms can also capture information and ideas.

From your website

Put a customer feedback form on your website, or instigate a customer careline service. Or you can simply encourage your customers to email you with their comments. Don't ignore these comments though, especially if you don't like what they're saying; this could be valuable and constructive criticism which could lead you to developing new products or adapting your existing ones.

From your competitors

Can you take some of your competitors' ideas and refine them, do them better or differently?

From published research

Read newspapers, magazines and trade articles, subscribe to the relevant online news services or conduct some research on the internet. This could all provide you with profitable ideas.

 ACTION POINT

- List your own products or services.
- What is the volume of sales generated for each product or service?
- Compare this with previous years' performance then plot your range of products or services on a lifecycle.
- Which products are in the maturity or growth phase of the product lifecycle?
- Which are in decline?
- What new products or services are being developed or introduced?

QUICK RECAP

- *Constantly develop new products and services to suit your existing customers, or for new customers.*
- *The product lifecycle explores the concept that products go through certain phases: introduction, growth, maturity and decline.*
- *Most companies have a range of products, each of which may be in a different stage of its lifecycle.*
- *The stage of your product or service will determine the marketing strategy, investment costs and profitability.*
- *You can extend the lifecycle and halt decline by **adapting the product**. This means taking an existing product or service and adapting it for an existing market, or for a completely new market.*
- *If sales are declining, you may decide to withdraw the product.*
- *Ideas for new products or services can come from talking and listening to your staff, talking and listening to your customers, from your competitors, published research and the media.*
- *Ask yourself if you are providing the right products and services to your customers in the best way.*

CHAPTER 5

Pricing

The prices for your goods or services will be dependent on a number of factors: your market, your product or service, your competitors and where your product or service is positioned in the product lifecycle. Pricing strategies will change. New entrants will come into your market, the attitudes of your customers can alter, technological breakthroughs will affect your product and therefore the cost of producing it and its positioning in the marketplace. You will need to constantly monitor your prices and adapt them accordingly. This chapter looks at the issues surrounding pricing and the various pricing strategies you can adopt.

SETTING PRICES

When looking at how you set your prices you need to consider the following:
- Your business objectives – how much profit do you wish to make and over what period?
- Your costs for producing the product or delivering the service.
- The competition. How many competitors do you have? What are they providing and what is their pricing strategy?
- What is the demand for your products or services?
- Do you have a distribution channel mark up?
- What discounts, if any, are you offering?

When setting your prices you may have a variety of objectives. Here are some of them:
- To earn a target on investment.
- To maximize short or long-term profit.
- To keep the business at a planned level of production or to keep staff employed.
- To achieve a certain amount of growth in a required period.
- To avoid government investigation and control.
- To enhance the image of the firm and its products or services.
- To help stabilise the market.
- To discourage entrants into the market.
- To meet or follow the competition.
- To stimulate cash recovery.
- To be regarded as fair by customers.
- To increase or maintain market share.

Obviously your business objectives can change and so too can your marketplace. Therefore, your prices will change to reflect this.

So what pricing strategies can you adopt? Most organisations use a variety of the ones I have listed below.

Price skimming
Your product or service may be so different that it represents a

drastic departure from the accepted ways of filling a demand or performing a service. You can therefore set a high price to skim or cream off the market before the product or service is replicated by others.

Q EXAMPLE

When the Dyson bagless vacuum cleaner came onto the market it was the first of its kind. It could therefore be priced higher than other vacuum cleaners. It could skim or cream off the market before its price became more sensitive as other copycat products entered the market. The higher prices can also help to recoup some of the outlay on research and development.

Market penetration

This is where low prices are used as an entering wedge to get into mass markets early.

Q EXAMPLE

Direct Line Insurance used this pricing strategy when entering the market. The company were unique in that it was the first to cut out the middle man (the broker) and sell insurance direct to the end user (the customer). However ,it decided not to use price skimming (setting a high price), but instead went in cheaper than the competition in order to gain market share, quickly.

Amazon.com is another example of this. When Amazon first came on to the scene in 1995, it was the first of its kind to fully exploit the potential of internet buying. It could easily have adopted a strategy of price skimming (charging a premium for the luxury of being able to order a book from the comfort of your own home and having it delivered direct to your door), but It didn't. Instead Amazon opted for lower prices and, at the same time, for excellence in customer service. The company pursued a strategy of rapid market penetration and then growth and is still, today, pursing a strategy of ambitious growth.

Strong potential competition is likely soon after the introduction of a new product or service when no 'elite' market, or no brand loyalty, exists and where people will respond to price.

Competitive pricing

You will set your prices to meet that of the competition.

Differential pricing

This is where you can charge different prices for the same product or service. This can be because of the different location of buyers, different types of customer or for large purchasers.

Q EXAMPLE

A management consultancy uses this pricing strategy. It sets lower daily rates for its small and medium-sized businesses which are based in the provinces, but higher rates for big corporations or the public sector and for those clients located in capital cities such as London where the cost of living is higher. It also has different pricing levels for working in different countries to reflect 'the going rate' in those countries. If it also has an established reputation for gaining results for its clients, through its commitment to employing talented and top-level consultants, its costs are higher – but its services are in demand and it can therefore set higher prices than its competitors.

Diversionary pricing

The actual price of the product or service is hidden in extras, ie installation, fitting etc. So although the price you might actually see says free delivery, or free installation, this cost is built into the actual cost of the product or service.

Dumping price

This is used to clean out excess obsolete stock. This technique can be seen in retail shops, in which old season stock that hasn't sold is drastically reduced to make room for the new season's wares.

The psychology of pricing

Price can sometimes be taken as an indication of quality, but if the price is perceived as being too high or too low then you may have to explain it or it will put people off.

🔍 EXAMPLE

When I worked for a wholesaler, a range of office equipment was reduced to ridiculously low prices. There was absolutely nothing wrong with the equipment; it wasn't even obsolete, but a genuine reduction. I watched as customers, initially attracted by the low prices, picked up the items and then put them down again. The goods were priced too cheaply. Customers thought there was something wrong with the products so they didn't buy.

TOP TIPS

People will also make a comparison between the product in terms of its 'perceived value', ie is it seen as value for money

Pricing can be linked to the packaging. Expensive packaging can associate the product in the eyes of the customers with expensive goods. Perfume is a good example of this, as are carrier bags from expensive shops.

Image can also play a part in the pricing game. A piece of pottery or porcelain in a tatty junk shop priced low may not be bought because it is perceived to be rubbish. Clean it up and put the same piece in an expensive antique shop and the price can be trebled (unless, of course, you have knowledge of antiques and know its true value).

People form expectations about the quality of a product based on its price.

TOP TIPS

You need to ask yourself if your price is right for your company image and for the products you sell or the services you deliver.

When might you need to look at price changes?

You will need to consider price changes for any of the following:

To help boost an ailing product

In the previous chapter I examined the product lifecycle and said that when a product starts to decline you may decide to repackage it and re-launch it. However, you may decide to lower the price of an ailing product in order to clear it out altogether, or you might run a 'special offer' for a period of time.

Loss leaders

This is a term more often associated with supermarkets. Wine and beer are sometimes used as loss leaders, as are books. This strategy will draw the customer into the shop and once there the customer will make other purchases. You could decide to sell your product or service at a low price and not actually make any profit on it because you know it will lead to further business or more sales from that customer. Many solicitors use their will-writing service as a loss leader. Some even write wills free of charge on the basis that once they write your will you will return to buy other legal services. If the solicitor is good at cross selling, this is often a very successful strategy.

To counter the competition

You may decide to lower your prices to counteract the activity of the competition. Here you need to be careful because any lowering of prices could lead to a downward spiral in the marketplace. Once prices have been driven down, it is extremely difficult to raise them again.

In a tough economic climate, with a declining or stagnant marketplace, you might decide to lower your prices in order to win more work and so retain your workforce. The problem with this is that it could not only lead to a price-cutting war, but it could also affect other products or services in the range. In addition, it could change a customer's perception towards you and lead to an image of financial instability. For example, those shops which permanently have a sale are in danger of being thought of as the low-quality option, teetering on the edge of collapse.

 ACTION POINT

• Examine your own pricing strategies: are they the correct ones?
• What are your objectives and how will this affect your pricing strategy?
• What is the image of your products/services and how are you perceived in the marketplace?
• Where are your products or services on the product lifecycle? Are they priced correctly to reflect this?

 QUICK RECAP

• *The prices you set at first won't stay the same forever.*
• *Be attuned to the marketplace, the competition and changing consumer attitudes.*
• *Price can sometimes be taken as an indication of quality.*
• *People will also make a comparison between the product and its 'perceived value'.*
• *Pricing can also be linked to the packaging.*
• *You should consider price changes when launching a new product, to help boost an ailing product and as a loss leader to counter competition.*

CHAPTER 6

Building a competitive edge

One of the biggest challenges for businesses today is working out how to build and maintain a competitive edge. There are a number of ways of doing this, all of which are very easy to say (or write) but most of which are difficult to carry out and sustain. In this chapter I examine some of the ways you can build a competitive edge for your business.

HOW TO BUILD A COMPETITIVE EDGE

Building a competitive edge for your organisation, its products and services can be done through the following means:
• Branding
• Image
• Price
• Product or service differentiation
• Building and maintaining an excellent reputation for providing a good service or product.

Or you could build a competitive edge for your products or services through a combination of the above. For example, Amazon has built a competitive edge through strong branding of the Amazon name, competitive pricing of its products, and building and maintaining an excellent reputation for service delivery.

Let's examine the above elements in greater detail.

BRANDING

Why brand?

What matters is not merely what people know about your product but how they feel about it and how it relates to their own personality and lifestyle. People tend to buy what they are familiar with. They like to know what the product or service stands for and whether or not it is the right one for them. Branding helps them to make this choice.

> Branding is used to define identity and helps people relate to the product.

Branding is used very strongly in the fast-moving consumer goods market (FMCG) where customer loyalty needs to be constantly fought for. It can also be used on other products, including industrial goods, and on books such as this, which follow a certain brand style. In the service sector, and in business-to-business markets, image, as an aspect of branding, is very important and I will look at this in more detail later.

Branding will give a product identity and make it more easily recognisable. If people know what a brand stands for, and where it fits with their own needs, it is easier for them to buy it.

People will ask:

- Does this brand fit my lifestyle?
- Does it express my identity?
- Is it value for money?
- How available is it?
- What do I think about it – do I like or dislike it?

Building a brand

Various factors go into building a brand. These include:

- The product itself
- The packaging
- The advertising
- The brand name
- The price
- How and where it is distributed
- Its availability
- Its logo, colours, style, any strap lines
- The consistency of communicating all the above, which goes into forming a corporate image or identity.

Branding also goes beyond this. Things such as quality, service, reliability, innovation and integrity all come into play. Branding is the result of a successful marketing and business strategy. It will reflect how you train your staff in the company's values and how you manage your relationships with your customers.

Choosing a brand name

This can be a very tricky area and marketing history is littered with expensive errors. Essentially though the brand name should:

• Never contradict the essential product qualities
• Not have unfortunate connotations
• Be easy to say, pronounce and catchy
• Fit onto the packaging.

 ACTION POINT

Take a look at some well-known brands and companies. What words do you associate with these brands or companies?

• Guinness
• Ford
• Mercedes
• Sony
• Nike
• Microsoft
• Kellogg's
• Virgin
• Heinz

Now ask someone in your company to do the same exercise and compare your findings. Did you come up with the same or similar brand images? If so then these companies are successfully communicating their brand image and values. Try summing up your company's products/services, brand values.

IMAGE

Building and maintaining a favourable image of your organisation in the minds and eyes of your customers is vital. The image of the company is an essential ingredient in the choice of services and often in the choice of products. But this image has to be managed. It doesn't just happen.

So what elements go into communicating an image and how can you manage this?

First impressions

All visitors to your company carry away with them an impression. You need to make sure it is the right impression. Whether it is on the telephone or face-to-face, first impressions count. Remember the saying 'You never get a second chance to make a first impression'? Well, this applies to **your organisation and your staff**. If the hotel I used in an earlier example has dirty curtains, peeling paintwork and scuffed flooring, or the receptionist or staff are unhelpful, then the first impressions won't be at all good. I certainly wouldn't wish to stay there and you might not either. Not only that but I would also tell others not to go there.

If a restaurant's toilets are dirty, then what are the kitchens like? I have often walked out of a restaurant after seeing the state of the toilets. And I'm not the only one to do so.

How does your company treat visitors – any visitors, not just potential customers but the person who comes to clean the windows or service the photocopier, the delivery drivers and suppliers? Remember every person carries away with them an impression of your company. They could all be potential customers, or they could have relatives and friends who could be potential customers.

Here is a checklist to see if your organisation is getting first impressions right. It covers key areas in making a first impression such as what your office and reception area looks like, the professionalism of your reception staff, the attitude of other staff with visitors, and how the telephone is answered.

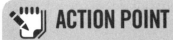 **ACTION POINT**

Tick if you've got the following right:

☐ Is the entrance to your organisation clean and tidy?

☐ Is the name of the organisation prominently displayed?

☐ Have the logo and corporate colours been used on the signs?

☐ Is the entrance door clearly marked Reception?

☐ Are the company brochures on display? Are they up to date and fresh looking?

☐ Is the reception area clean, tidy and uncluttered?

☐ Is there somewhere for people to sit and wait in comfort?

☐ Is the receptionist dressed smartly or in a uniform provided?

☐ Does the receptionist smile on greeting a visitor?

☐ Does the receptionist ask the visitor's name and use it?

☐ Does the receptionist invite the visitor to take a seat?

☐ Does the receptionist offer the visitor a cup of tea or coffee?

☐ If there is a delay does the receptionist keep the visitor informed?

☐ Does the receptionist give good eye contact with the visitor?

When a staff member meets the visitor:

☐ Is the visitor greeted with a smile and the use of their name?

☐ Does the staff member shake hands with the visitor?

☐ Does the staff member open friendly conversation?

When the interview has finished:

☐ Does the staff member show the visitor out?

☐ Does the staff member shake hands, smile and thank them?

How is the telephone answered?

☐ Is the telephone answered within three rings?

☐ If not, what is the procedure if the telephone rings more than this?

☐ Is the telephone answered with the organisation's or staff member's name?

☐ Is there a message-taking policy if the person is not available?

> Remember first impressions count. Make sure it is the correct impression. Take time to get all these vital elements right.

Reception areas can be a hazard zone. They can often descend into areas where the staff congregate to gossip. Here is what happened to me once:

I was sitting in the reception area of a very large international company waiting to see the commercial director, when two women decided to do the most wonderful (or rather I should say awful) character assassination on the man I was to meet. I learnt a great deal about him, not all of it true, I'm sure! But it certainly gave me enough information to know the personality I was about to meet and therefore how to approach him. Make sure that receptions aren't gossip zones in your organisation.

There are other elements that go into communicating an image and here I have listed some of them.

Your media coverage
Is it favourable or unfavourable, or non-existent?

Sponsorship
If you undertake sponsorship, how is your company name seen in the light of the sponsorship? Is it the right image?

Brochures/leaflets/newsletters
How is your name and company image portrayed on your marketing material?

Advertising
What image are you portraying through your advertising? Is it strong enough? Does it say what your company stands for? Do your staff advertisements communicate to potential recruits the image of your organisation?

Stationery

From your letterheads to your fax cover sheets and emails, what image are you communicating to your customers? Is your letterhead too fussy or out of date? Are you using up old supplies of stationery with old logos and designs whilst at the same time using new stationery with new designs? If you are, then your target markets are receiving mixed messages.

Your staff

What is the general attitude and appearance of your staff? Do they know what image your organisation wishes to portray to its markets? If they don't, how can they possibly communicate this? Do they wear a uniform, and if so what does this say about the organisation?

Your vehicles

The appearance of your vans, cars and lorries is important in communicating an image. If a van, or car, displaying your company name is badly driven then what does this say about your company? If the van or lorry is dirty and falling to pieces, what image is your organisation projecting? A pretty bad one, don't you think!

Signage

If your company signage, both external and internal, is tatty, dirty or badly displayed it doesn't do much for image.

Your website

Is this communicating the correct image for your company – not only through its design but by its ease of use and the services it offers? Is it fully available or does the server keep going off line? Is it written in the language your target markets would respond to? What graphics are you using and do they appeal to your target customers? Do all the elements of the website come together to match the image you wish to convey, be that traditional and safe, modern and creative or somewhere in between?

TOP TIPS

The Petty Matters matter! Take time to get all the things that go into making an image right and keep checking they are right.

COMPETITIVE EDGE THROUGH PRICE

Another and perhaps obvious way of building a competitive edge is through **price**. However, this may not necessarily be the best way. You can be cheaper than the competition and so gain market share, but market share is not everything if sacrificed on the altar of profitability. Remember that once your prices are lowered it is difficult to raise them again. In addition, you need to consider what image you wish to portray to your customers – cheap and cheerful, or value for money? It all depends on what market you are in and how your customers perceive you, the product or service, and its price.

Conversely you could charge a premium price and build a competitive edge this way. Perhaps you have an excellent image and reputation and this is taken into account when customers decide to buy from you.

Price isn't everything and can often be of secondary consideration when quality and reputation are strong.

COMPETITIVE DIFFERENTIATION

You may have a product or a service that is very different from your competitors and therefore be able to gain a competitive edge. They say that imitation is the highest form of flattery and you can bet your bottom dollar that if you're doing something unique, or have a unique product, it won't remain unique for long. If it's good, imitators will come into your market, therefore making product or service differentiation very hard to maintain.

Innovation is important. You should be constantly looking for new and better ways to deliver a service, or be searching for a better, more improved product.

TOP TIPS

THE IMPORTANCE OF REPUTATION

All the money you spend on marketing will be wasted if you don't get things right inside your organisation. If you have worked hard to win the customer and then things go wrong as soon as the customer buys from you, you might as well throw your money away.

Do good work and more work comes from it.

Having an excellent reputation in your field of expertise, or for your products, is the best way of building a competitive edge. But building a good reputation can take years of painstaking hard work and only months, maybe even weeks, to destroy if you are not careful.

Building and maintaining a good reputation has to be worked at – constantly. No person, and no one organisation, can afford to be complacent. If you or your organisation becomes complacent then it is almost guaranteed that you will lose business and one of your most precious business assets: your good name.

The importance of staff

Your staff are vital when it comes to maintaining a good reputation. In a service organisation at least 90% of the staff will come into direct contact with the customer. They may even deliver the service and, as people buy people, so your customers will be making buying decisions based on whether or not they like the people in your company. If they don't like them, they won't buy from them. In service organisations, marketing strategies and personnel strategies cannot be separated from each other. Therefore getting the right people and retaining them is absolutely vital.

If you are marketing a product rather than a service, aren't staff just as important? Of course, few of the staff will come into direct contact with the customer but they all have a part to play in getting that product out of the factory gate on time and to the right standard. They rely on each other to do jobs efficiently and effectively.

If you have staff who couldn't care less, or who simply come in to work, do their bit and then disappear as quickly as possible without being motivated by you, then their attitude will undoubtedly affect your competitive edge.

Remember that marketing orientation checklist in Chapter 1? Well, you want your staff working with you, not against you, and to do this they have to share the same vision as you. Your staff need to know what your organisation stands for, so define it and communicate it, consistently, not only through the written word but also through leading by example.

> Define excellence and make it your objective.

Ensure that excellence is led from the TOP. This means the business owner, director and manager. If it isn't, it will fail.

Set standards of how you expect your staff to behave. And make sure you adhere to those standards yourself.

Ensure that if you have a dress and behaviour code that it is fair and consistent. You can't have one standard of behaviour and dress for your staff and a different standard for yourself or the management. When you draw up a behaviour or dress code make sure you involve your staff in this. These are usually highly contentious areas and can cause a great deal of friction. If staff are involved then they are more committed to making it work. Make sure you communicate these standards. Ensure that all your staff are clear on what is expected of them.

You will also need to examine training needs, and issues like staff incentives. Give your staff a real sense of personal responsibility and try to develop an environment in which orders can be passed and carried out effectively.

Also give staff a sense of belonging: make them feel informed and involved. Ensure that they have a share in the success of the organisation.

In order to ensure you have a well-motivated workforce you must be concerned with their personal wants, needs and desires. There are no bad companies, only bad managers. So you must make time to get staff relations right and continually work at it. It will pay dividends for the business if you have a happy, well-motivated workforce and it *will* contribute directly to the bottom-line profit. Remember, I also said that you can get ideas for improving services or products from staff. So get their feedback and do this on a continuous basis.

Give your staff the training they need, not only for them to be able to do their jobs, but also in people handling skills. And plan for continuing training.

Make sure you measure and monitor performance. This can be done through regular and valued performance reviews or appraisals. Ensure that the staff members doing the appraisals are trained in how to do this and that the system is confidential and fair.

Don't forget to reward your staff. This does not necessarily mean a pay rise (although I am sure they would always welcome one!) but often a 'thank you' or 'well done' is enough. Too many of us are too ready to criticise and forget to give praise when it is deserved. People are motivated through praise, not punishment.

Reward people through giving them extra responsibility or a different project. Training and development can also be motivating and rewarding. Above all, recruit the right people with the right attitude.

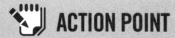 **ACTION POINT**

- Examine your products and services. Have you developed a strong brand for them?
- Does your organisation have strong branding?
- Write down what that brand image is and then get your staff and customers to tell you what they think it is. Do you come up with the same points?
- Conduct the first impressions checklists and identify areas that need to be put right. Make a list of them and say how you are going to put them right and when.
- If you employ staff, carry out a staff audit. How happy and motivated are your staff? Examine their training needs and look at how you can improve the motivation of your staff.
- Put a communications strategy in place to keep your staff informed and involved.

QUICK RECAP

- There are a number of ways you can build a competitive edge but the key to doing so and maintaining a competitive edge is consistency.
- You can build a competitive edge through: branding, image, price, product or service differentiation and by having a reputation for excellence.
- Branding is used to define identity and helps people relate to the product.
- People will ask themselves if the brand fits with their lifestyle and identity, whether or not it is value for money.
- Various factors go into making up a brand image. These include the product itself, the packaging, the advertising, the brand name, the price, how and where it is distributed and its availability.
- Having a clearly defined image for your business, products or services will greatly enhance your organisation's competitiveness and increase sales.
- Building a good reputation for excellence in your field will ensure you get recommendations and repeat business.
- First impressions can be critical. Make sure they are the right impressions.
- When building a competitive edge, your staff are vital.
- Ensure that everyone is working for the organisation, not against it.
- Develop a personality for your organisation and lead it from the TOP.
- Set standards for how you expect your staff to behave.

CHAPTER 7

Marketing planning

So you know who your customers are, and you know your products and services. You've examined how to build a competitive edge and you've analysed your products or services and your pricing strategies. So where do you go from here? This chapter looks at making sure you have a database to capture and analyse information, how to analyse your organisation's strengths and weaknesses (SW) and opportunities and threats (OT), and how to set your objectives and develop your marketing strategies.

YOUR DATABASE

A database is a vital marketing and management information tool for driving your business forward. Many organisations have one, but not all pay attention to maintaining them and utilising them to the full. Your database should contain:

- Information about your existing customers and their transactions, ie what they have bought over a period of time and when.
- Details about the decision making process of your customers, ie who buys and their position. This is particularly relevant in business markets.
- Details of how the customer heard of you, eg advertising, mailshot, e-shot, recommendation, press item, etc.
- The value and volume of sales per customer.
- If a representative visits customers, or a telemarketing person calls them, make sure the date and result of the call, or the visit, is logged and the date of the next call is flagged up.
- A brief history of the customer.
- A breakdown of your customers and prospects by industry type, geographical area, number of employees etc, or by consumer type and background information.
- A list of potential customers and details on them.
- The history of contact with the company.
- The history of marketing activities with which they've been targeted.

You should also use the database to review past customers. If someone has bought from you once and then stopped buying from you, you need to find out why, and win that customer back. If you have done something to upset them then you want to know about it. You can only put things right if you listen to your customers, accept their comments, and then act on them.

If you are receiving enquiries from your website, make sure it has a database function and can transfer names and addresses captured online. Customers or prospects can then be emailed or sent personalised marketing material. Online buying (e-commerce) sites should have this function as a matter of course. You should also include an enquiry form which has a prompt asking how the customer heard of you. This information can then be analysed and any pattern of buying identified. It will also help you to monitor the effectiveness of your marketing activity. (More on website analysis in Chapter 13.)

TOP TIPS

A database will help you:

■ Track developments in your customer base

■ Identify prospects and their potential to buy

■ Target key customers and prospects with the right messages

■ Monitor the success or otherwise of your marketing activity

■ Identify areas of improvements eg customer care: what problems and complaints are you regularly receiving?

■ Monitor sales and decline of sales of products/ services.

If you don't have a database, or use it properly, all your forecasts will be based on highly suspect, historical data.

SWOT ANALYSIS

A SWOT analysis is an analysis of the strengths, weaknesses, opportunities and threats that your business currently faces. The SWOT analysis should be conducted at least twice yearly and your marketing plan should address the weaknesses identified in your organisation and build on its strengths. It should also state how you are going to capitalise on any opportunities and what action you are going to take to overcome any threats to the business.

The strengths and weaknesses focus on the **internal** aspects of your business. The opportunities and threats are the **external** aspects and therefore, to a certain degree, are outside your control. These cover the political, environmental, social and technological (PEST) activities in the outside world that have an impact on a business.

An example SWOT could look like this:

Strengths	Weaknesses
Good customer base	Weak in developing new products for customers
Good product range	Website out of date
Well-motivated staff	Reception area needs updating
	Some products beginning to decline
	No new product development
Opportunities	**Threats**
Growth in older population creating new opportunities for us	Higher interest rates could affect consumer spending
Internet use increasing, therefore opening up possible new markets for us	Change of government could affect legislation in our markets
Some competitors closing down	New competitors entering market

The same item could appear under both columns. For example, legislation introduced by the government could pose both a threat and an opportunity to your organisation. The competition could also be both a threat and an opportunity, ie you might be able to take market share from your competitors, but equally they could take market share from you.

Looking at the big picture like this will help you identify how you can grow and in which areas you need to develop.

Other things that need to be considered under opportunities and threats are discussed in the following sections.

Consumer changes

Changes in consumer attitudes, lifestyles, habits, values and trends occur regularly. How will these affect your business? Identifying gaps in the market for new products and services could identify an impending change in consumer patterns. Our lifestyle today is much faster than that of previous generations. Customers want their products delivered quickly, hence the growth of same-day delivery services. Those organisations that spot the opportunities presented by changing consumer attitudes will continue to gain a competitive advantage and win market share.

Technological developments

How will technology impact on your business? Digital television is set to open up new markets and change buying habits. E-commerce is a reality. Social networks are booming and thriving. Mobile technology or communication on the move is increasingly popular. Can your organisation embrace it and exploit it as an opportunity to reach new markets, or are your competitors leaving you behind? How will technology change the way your business operates? Will it save you money, increase your ability to serve customers or enable you to produce goods more quickly? How will it change the way your customers choose a supplier or buy goods?

Legislation

Perhaps new legislation will open up a new market for you, but it could also seriously affect the viability of a business and its markets.

Economic changes

Recession, recovery, interest rate increases or decreases. How much money do people or businesses have to spend or invest? How will this affect your company's performance?

ACTION POINT

Conduct a thorough SWOT analysis for your organisation.

• Involve your staff in this exercise. Ask them to come up with a SWOT analysis.

• Compare the two – do they come up with the same SWOT analysis as you?

• Consider engaging outside consultants and advisers to help you. People outside an organisation can often see things that those inside are too close to spot. They can sometimes be more objective.

Everything I have covered so far is information required for drawing up your **marketing plan**, covered in detail in Chapter 17. To recap, you need to identify your customers and potential customers, understand your marketplace, analyse your products and pricing strategies, look at how you can build and sustain a competitive edge and conduct a SWOT analysis. The next step is to set your marketing objectives and identify your marketing strategies.

SETTING MARKETING OBJECTIVES

When setting your objectives, it is not enough to say that you want to be the best company in town, because how are you going to measure that? How do you know when you are the best? Your objectives, therefore, have to be specific and measurable. They need to be achievable, realistic and timed. In short, they need to be **SMART**.

SMART stands for:
Specific
Measurable
Achievable
Realistic
Timed

Example objectives:

- To increase market share of X product/service from 10% to 20% of the current market by January 20XX.
- To increase sales of X product/service from £1.8m to £2m by January 20XX.
- To maintain X% profitability levels on X product range over the year.
- To investigate at least two new markets and to identify one key market to penetrate in 20XX.

Whatever your objectives, ensure they are realistic and achievable. If you set them too high, or have too many, then they will be difficult to achieve and this only becomes demotivating.

TOP TIPS

Questions to be asked:

- Are your products or services meeting customer needs properly?
- Do all your products or services optimise sales and profit?
- Are your resources being utilised to the full, ie raw materials, plant, labour, etc?
- What are your competitors doing?
- What are the opportunities and threats created by regulations?
- What are the opportunities and threats created by changing market conditions?

With these points in mind let's look at what marketing strategies you can adopt. We'll start by looking at market penetration, then at how you can develop your product or service, then move on to extending your market and diversification of your products.

MARKETING STRATEGIES

There are four basic marketing strategies.

1. Market penetration

This involves keeping your existing customers and finding new ones. For example, the printer in our previous example might have auctioneers and mail order companies as existing clients, and because these types of client are highly profitable, it would make good sense for him to find more of them.

2. Product or service development

This involves improving your existing products or services, ie improving the quality, adapting the style, offering something new for your existing customers.

For example, our printer has decided to expand the services he offers to include multi-channel marketing solutions for his existing customers. This means that he not only offers to print their brochures, newsletter and flyers, but he can also offer an emailing service and web-based ordering.

3. Market extension

This involves finding new markets for your existing products or services, ie going further afield geographically, or appealing to a new group or type of customer.

Here, the printer, after analysing his customer base and the marketplace, decides that a new and potentially good market would be to expand into the training sector where he can print training manuals. He can also consider expanding from his current geographical area into a new one.

4. Diversification

This involves increasing your sales by developing new products for new markets.

This final strategy carries the highest cost and the highest risk. You are entering a market you know nothing about, with a product or service you have no experience of.

Businesses usually adopt a combination of the first three strategies to achieve their objectives.

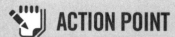

ACTION POINT

- Set your objectives for the next year at least, or review the ones you have already set. Are they SMART?
- Identify the marketing strategies you are going to use to help you achieve your objectives.

QUICK RECAP

- *A database is a vital marketing and management information tool for driving your business forward.*
- *It should record existing customers and their transactions, and review past customer transactions.*
- *It can be used to personalise your mailings, newsletters and brochures, and to send out regular e-bulletins and e-newsletters.*
- *A database will help to identify prospects and their buying potential, target key customers and prospects with the right messages, monitor the success or otherwise of your marketing activity, identify areas of improvements, monitor sales and decline of sales of products or services.*
- *The SWOT analysis should be conducted at least twice yearly.*
- *Your marketing plan should address the weaknesses identified in your organisation and build on its strengths.*
- *Marketing objectives should be specific, measurable, achievable, realistic and timed (SMART).*
- *Don't set too many objectives because if you can't fulfil them you will become de-motivated.*
- *There are four basic marketing strategies to help you achieve your objectives: market penetration, product/ service development, market extension, diversification.*

PART 2

USING MARKETING TECHNIQUES

CHAPTER 8

The marketing tools

Having gained a clear direction of where you are heading and who you are targeting, you need to identify the right marketing or promotional tools to reach those target customers. This chapter looks at the marketing tools at your disposal and the following chapters cover these techniques in depth to show you how you can use these more effectively.

TOP TIPS

People can't buy from you unless they know you exist.

So you need to communicate with them. You need to tell them you exist! There are a number of ways you can do this and a number of promotional tools you can use. You have to decide which tools, or what mix of tools, are the best. This will depend on:

- What you are hoping to achieve, ie your objectives
- What budget you have set
- Whether or not it is the appropriate method for that particular group of customers.

Here are some of the promotional tools you can use. The following chapters give you advice and guidance on how to use them.

SOME PROMOTIONAL TOOLS

Advertising
- Television
- Radio
- Newspapers
- Magazines
- Directories
- Wall planners, diaries etc
- Poster advertising, eg hoardings, railway platforms, bus shelters, buses etc
- Internet

Signage
- Business premises
- Cars, vans etc

Promotional items
- Notepads
- Pens

- Carrier bags
- T-shirts etc

Direct marketing

- Mail order catalogues
- 'Off the page' advertising
- Direct response advertising
- Mailshot letters
- Mailshot leaflets
- Door-drop leaflets
- Inserts into magazines
- Telemarketing
- Internet

E-marketing/viral marketing

- E-shots
- E-bulletins
- E-newsletters
- E-zines
- Social networking sites
- Blogs

Editorial

- Press releases and articles

Exhibitions and trade fairs

Personal selling

- Having a sales representative on the road and calling on prospects

Seminars/demonstrations/open days

Corporate hospitality

Sponsorship

Sales promotion techniques

- Merchandising – making sure your product is displayed to the maximum effect
- Giving special offers, eg two for the price of one, discounts, 10% extra etc
- Joint promotions – linking up with someone else

Personal recommendations

Much of your business should be generated through existing customers who come back to you and buy more from you, or who recommend you to others. Getting it right inside the organisation – your internal marketing – is extremely important.

You may be able to think of other promotional tools you can use to target your customers.

ESSENTIAL QUESTIONS

Before you decide to use any of the promotional tools, you should stop and ask the following questions. They will help you clarify how to get the best results.

> Always ask yourself whether or not this promotional activity will reach your target market.

1. What is my objective?

Be clear about what you are trying to achieve from the outset. For example, you may be advertising to stimulate sales and prompt enquiries. Alternatively, you may be advertising with the purpose of raising name awareness only amongst your target audience. This is a very different objective. It might not directly stimulate enquiries in the short term, but it could benefit you long term, especially if carried out consistently and in conjunction with other promotional tools.

A seminar could increase your organisation's profile in its target market, but you may not receive any enquiries at the seminar itself.

Only later, after you have followed up the contacts by a direct mail letter, telemarketing call, email, brochure and even possibly a special offer, do you see the full benefits of the seminar.

You may be carrying out a direct mail campaign with the objective of increasing your database. Once you have names on your database you can then begin to communicate with these prospects on a regular basis, perhaps through telemarketing, inviting them to a seminar or exhibition, sending them special promotions, and of course keeping in touch with them through your newsletter, e-newsletter and e-bulletins.

You may be attending an exhibition, not with the primary purpose of getting orders or leads, but because your competitors and the exhibition visitors may think you've gone out of business or that you're in financial difficulties if you are not there!

These are just some examples. The main message is to know what it is you are hoping to achieve, because only then will you be able to measure the success of it. And, of course, you must always track results.

2. What's the best way to communicate my message?

How are you going to communicate your message through this promotional tool? Don't forget you must communicate the benefits of what you are offering, in the language that the target market understands and can relate to.

You must also look at the image you are portraying, and brand values if appropriate. How are these being communicated with regard to the promotional tool you are using?

You will need to think about your target customers and how they will react to the message. How do you wish them to react? Define this and check back that you are achieving it.

3. What's the best promotional tools for my audience?

Have you chosen the right promotional tool to reach the right target audience? Remember back to Chapter 2 when we looked at what markets we are in.

4. How am I going to follow this through?

The key to successful marketing is consistency – consistently putting out the right message to the right target audience. People buy what they are familiar with, so you need to keep your company name, and/or your products or services, in front of your target customers on a regular basis. It is not enough to advertise once and then say, 'well that didn't work on to the next thing.' You will need to build awareness for your products or services over a period of time, through a campaign. This could be by advertising, using direct marketing, email, through the press or through all of these.

FAILURE OF BUSINESS MARKETING

Why do businesses fail in their marketing?
This is mainly due to three things:

1. They don't understand what markets they are really in and therefore try to be everything to all people.
2. They don't understand why their customers buy from them, and therefore they don't communicate the right messages.
3. They flit from one promotional tool to another, not giving any of them enough time to work.

Make sure this doesn't happen to you.

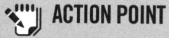 **ACTION POINT**

- Look at the markets you are targeting.

- What promotional methods are you going to use to reach them and communicate with them? Are they the right promotional tools?

- What is your objective in that target market?

- Will that promotional tool achieve that objective?

- Write down who you are going to target and say how (you might wish to come back to this point after reading the rest of this book).

- Identify what message might be the best to use – examine your features and benefits for the products and services you wish to promote and pick out the key benefits that will appeal to that target group.

- Remember to also consider why those customers will buy from you – the psychological factors.

QUICK RECAP

• *There are a number of promotional tools you can use. You have to decide which tools, or which mix of tools, are the most appropriate.*

• *You will need to consider what you are hoping to achieve, what your budget is and whether or not it is the most appropriate method for that particular group of customers.*

• *Before you decide to use any promotional tools, you should ask: can demand for this product or service be stimulated by using this promotional tool?*

• *Always track results.*

• *You must communicate the benefits of what you are offering, in the language that the target market understands and can relate to.*

• *You must also communicate your image and/or the brand values if appropriate.*

• *Be consistent in your approach.*

CHAPTER 9

Advertising

Advertising doesn't only apply to taking space in a newspaper or magazine, or running a campaign on the radio and television, or on the internet. It covers a variety of different areas. In this chapter I examine where you can advertise and how you can make your advertising more effective to boost results.

First, before deciding whether or not to advertise, you need to address the questions that I posed in the previous chapter:

- What is my objective?
- Who am I targeting?
- Will this form of advertising reach these target groups?
- Is advertising something they would respond to?
- How can my message be creatively different?

So let's look at the objectives for advertising.

ADVERTISING OBJECTIVES

- To build demand for your product or service on launch
- To give the customer details about and instructions on how to use a product
- To build brand recognition for your product
- To create a certain image for the brand, or for the company
- To give information about a price promotion and so stimulate demand
- To build names and addresses on the database
- To educate people, eg drink driving campaigns, no smoking campaigns
- To back up sales drives
- To drive visitors to your website
- To influence consumers to buy.

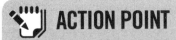 **ACTION POINT**

Ask yourself the following questions before advertising:

1. Who buys my product or service?
2. Why do they buy it? What is it used for?
3. What is the extent of advertising needed to reach this target group of customers?
4. How much do I need to do to get the message across?
5. What media are my target customers exposed to?
6. What do I know about the media?

All of these questions need to be taken into account when looking at the following media.

ADVERTISING MEDIA

Printed media

Printed media include magazines, newspapers, directories, wall planners, diaries. If you decide to advertise in a printed publication, try to obtain a copy of it beforehand, or look up the details on the internet, where the majority of publications now have a presence. If, however, you are advertising in a local directory, on a wall planner, or something similar, there might not be an appropriate website giving you details of the publication. In this case, ask to see a copy of a previous publication before you decide whether or not to advertise. You need to ask yourself the following questions:

- Would this publication attract my customers?
- Who else is advertising in it?
- Are any of my competitors advertising, and if so, does this mean we should or shouldn't?
- Are there complementary products and services on offer? You could try telephoning a couple of the advertisers (but probably not your competitors) to ask about their response.
- What is the content of the editorial (if any), and would it appeal to my target customers?
- Would my target customers buy/read/use/see this publication?
- What are the circulation figures and the readership? (You might be able to view this on the publication's website.)
- How often is the magazine/newspaper/directory/wall planner published?
- What are the rates, the copy deadlines and what special deals will they do for me?

You might also consider linking printed advertising with online advertising on that publication's website. This could be effective, but it depends on the publication and your target audience. You might have one group of customers who only read online publications, another who prefer to have the printed version and a third that view both.

In order to obtain costs and relevant information about a publication, you should be able to download a media pack from the advertiser's website (unless you are dealing with very small and local publications, in which case ask them for full costs and readership figures).

In addition, does the publication have a forthcoming feature list and do the planned feature articles fit with your products and services?

TOP TIPS

You might wish to consider advertising around a special feature, or see if you could get some editorial into the publication during that feature.

Most media packs and publications' websites provide details of their core target audience, which will help you to match it against your target customers.

Broadcast media

Check if this is the right media for your products and services. Ask the radio or television station for audience figures, and how far their audience reaches. Obtain information about the programme's type of audience, for example their age and socioeconomic background. Who listens to or watches that programme – are they your target audience? When and how do your target audience listen to the radio station? For example, is this in the car on their way to and from work, or at work or home? What time of day do they listen? This will obviously dictate the best time for you to run an advertising campaign.

Who else is advertising on that radio station or television channel? Are they your competitors or do their products or services fit well with yours? What is the cost of advertising (including the cost of producing the advertisement) and how long will you need to run the campaign in order to get your target audience to respond?

Poster advertising

Poster advertising includes hoardings, railway station platforms, bus shelters, buses, ad vans and mobile billboards. Poster and billboard advertising doesn't have to be national; you can tailor this to where your customers are based. Most poster advertising is handled by specialist companies, or advertising and marketing agencies. They will be able to search for the best providers of these services, and negotiate space and cost on your behalf. They will also be able to design a poster, or series of posters, and advise on how best to get your message across.

Alternatively you can search for companies on the internet who specialise in this area, who will provide you with information on locations, poster production and costs.

Are there any other places where you might legitimately be able to advertise your organisation? Think about your products or services and target customers, where do they visit, drive? What do they see? Are there opportunities to advertise, or to place a sign in that location?

Advertising can appear in a variety of locations and some unusual places. For example, in Britain, advertisements can be found on roundabouts and on the back of toilet doors in motorway service stations. I've even seen adverts on a herd of cows in a field beside a motorway!

Internet advertising

There are a huge number of internet sites advertising and selling goods and services. The advent of broadband technology and the ability to access websites through mobile communications and wireless technology has made this a truly mobile, flexible and cost-effective way to market goods.

You can advertise your products or services on your own website, as well as with search engines such as Google and Yahoo!, which also have links to social networking sites and mobile communication platforms. As the web is able to analyse traffic to a site, behavioural targeting means you can tailor your campaigns to reach your target audience taking into account their demographics, where they live and their interests. This is based on the internet users' claimed interest and activity when they undertake a search and click through to certain websites, or pages on a website.

You could consider advertising with pay-per-click campaigns with Google Adwords or Yahoo! Search Marketing and Microsoft AdCenters. You can set your budgets without worrying about overspending – but do keep a careful check on this and make sure that you are advertising the correct keywords (more about this in Chapter 13.)

You can also advertise on social networking sites such as Facebook and MySpace, one of the fastest internet growth areas.

Remember the same rules that apply to other forms of advertising also apply to electronic advertising: it is unfair, illegal and unethical to deceive customers and misrepresent services and goods.

Mobile marketing and advertising

Mobile marketing, and advertising via mobile phones is a developing and fast growing area. It has particular appeal to a generation that has grown up on mobile communications and to those whose jobs and lifestyles involve constant travelling. The mobile is direct, personal, interactive and targeted; able to reach the customer wherever he goes. Text messaging is now a recognised cultural phenomenon.

The benefit of using mobile marketing is its personalised nature.

The downside is that with increased use, customers could come to view your messages as spam. As with all marketing, it needs to be targeted and relevant. The campaign, offer or advertisement needs to be tailored to suit your customers. You also need their permission to communicate with them in this manner. You can build your own list by asking customers for their permission to contact them via this medium, or you can acquire names of those individuals who have given their permission to be reached by mobile marketing through a reputable mailing house. Mobile advertising works best when engaging the consumer in a two-way dialogue, and when reinforced by other marketing, for example also advertising on the internet or sending an e-shot. This form of advertising requires a high degree of interactivity, so look at ways that you can engage the customer – through competitions, text-based games and images. However, don't over-complicate things. The message must be simple, creative and intuitive.

Q EXAMPLE

The Salvation Army decided to try out mobile marketing for a new donation campaign in the USA for Christmas 2008. As well as using its standard methods of ringing bells and collecting in red kettles, the charity tested out advertising for donations via text messaging. Donors were sent text messages giving details of a dedicated number for them to donate to the charity.

Key rules for mobile marketing

- Mobile communications are personal rather than work-based.
- It is a direct form of communication with the individual.
- Beware of invading someone's personal space – think how the message can be made to relate to the individual.
- Be creative in your message.
- Be interactive; engage in a dialogue.
- Use imagery.

- Get the individual's permission to communicate with him in this way.
- Make it clear to the consumer how often and in what circumstances you will communicate with him.
- Give him a way to opt out.
- Clearly indicate who the message is from.

Before embarking on a mobile marketing campaign, check out the regulations in your own country. In the UK, three sets of regulations come into play with mobile marketing: the Data Protection Act, the Mobile Marketing Association (MMA) code of conduct and the New Electronic Communications Directive. You can also see how mobile marketing works with sales promotion techniques in Chapter 15.

'Off the page' advertising

'Off the page' advertisements appear in many magazines and newspapers. Customers can buy the product 'off the page', paying by cheque or credit card, either by using the coupon response or by telephoning to place their order. Here, then, you need to display your product advert in the most appropriate publication, ie one that reaches your target customers. You might also wish to consider outsourcing fulfilment to a specialist company if you expect the response to be high, or if you do not have adequate in-house resources to handle it.

Direct response advertising

Many products and services are sold direct through advertising on the television or radio. Often a freephone telephone number, or low-cost number, is provided. Charities effectively raise thousands of pounds through their direct response advertising campaigns targeted at key times throughout the year, for example at Christmas. With direct response advertising the customer calls the telephone number given and pays for the product via a credit or debit card. You need to carefully match your target customer with the target media. You will also need to ensure that your organisation, or the outsourced call centre, can handle the response to a campaign.

Direct marketing

Mailshot letters, leaflets, inserts in magazines, flyers and door-drop leaflets are generally known as **direct marketing** because you are communicating with your audience directly, rather than through an intermediary. However, when writing and designing a mailshot campaign (including letters, leaflets, door drops and inserts into magazines and newspapers), the rules of good advertising apply, which is why I have included it here. Those rules of good advertising are covered in the following chapter. Well-targeted and well-designed mailshots, tailored and personalised to the customer, can be an extremely successful form of marketing. They are controllable and the results can be measured. Find out how to write a mailshot in Chapter 10.

Signage

Don't overlook the opportunity to boost your organisation's profile through obvious signage like that on your vehicles, business property and staff uniforms. Of course this is not relevant to every business, but signage and uniforms are a positive marketing tool when it comes to marketing a service, or helping to reinforce brand identity and image. If you are advertising on your company vehicles, consider the image and impression your drivers are making on the public. A cleaning company with dirty vans is not a good advertisement, and reckless and rude drivers can severely damage an organisation's reputation and therefore lose vital sales.

E-shots

E-shots are the same as mailshots except you are using email to send your advertising offer to a recipient rather than using the postal system. E-shots are a direct form of marketing, where you are targeting customers direct. As with direct mail and mobile marketing it is best that you check out the rules and regulations regarding the sending of e-shots in your country or the country you are targeting before embarking on a campaign, because different countries have different legislation covering this. This is covered in more detail in Chapter 11.

Promotional items

Promoting your organisation's name and key marketing message through certain promotional items that are often given away for free can help to spread the word and reinforce brand name and image. They won't stimulate sales on their own, but coupled with other marketing activity they could help to keep your organisation's name in front of your target customers on an ongoing basis.

Whichever media you choose, ensure that all the media details match with your target audience. Be clear about your objectives for advertising.

QUICK RECAP

Before deciding whether or not to advertise you need to be clear:

- *What your objective is*
- *Who you are targeting*
- *Whether the chosen form of advertising will reach your target customers*
- *Whether they will respond to it*
- *How your message can be creatively different.*

CHAPTER 10

How to make advertising and mailshots work

It's all very well taking advertising space, or deciding to run a mailing campaign, but simply stringing a few words together and adding a 'nice' picture won't get customers flocking to buy your products and services. The consumer today is bombarded with tons of advertising messages, so you need to make yours stand out to get results. This chapter examines how you can do this.

In order to be effective, advertising (including direct mail) must create a sense of familiarity with the target audience.

TOP TIPS

In order for adverts and direct mail to work they must be:

- Seen
- Read
- Remembered
- Believed
- Acted upon.

Successful advertising also needs to fulfil the following criteria:

1. Awareness of the brand or company

The customer must be *aware* of the brand or company. In order to build awareness, you need to advertise over a period of time, and/or advertise in a number of different media at the same time. Alternatively, you might mix your promotional tools, for example while running an advertising campaign in a publication, you might also run a direct mail campaign, coupled with some editorial in relevant magazines, along with online advertising or an email campaign. This way, the prospect becomes more aware of your company/brand across a range of media to which they are exposed.

2. Understanding of the product

There must be some *understanding* of what the product is and what it will do for the customer. This means that your message must explain clearly and succinctly how buying the product/ brand/service will **benefit** the customer.

3. Conviction to buy

The customer must arrive at the mental *conviction* to buy the product. Your message must also carry a genuine attractiveness that convinces the customer he must have it, so a clear understanding of what your customer wants is paramount.

4. Customer action

The customer must stir himself into *action*. You ne
customer saying, 'Yes, I must have that.' And you ne
easy for him to buy.

Advertising and direct mailing regulations can vary from
country to country so always make sure that you comply with
the law. In some countries, advertising is very prominent, while
in others it is practically non-existent. So, again, it is a question
of understanding your target audience and knowing the best
methods to reach them. In addition, certain products may be
banned from being advertised, such as cigarettes in the UK. And
there is, of course, the question of advertising in the language
of the country: does your product name and advertising message
need to change to make sense and appeal to the right people?

MAKING AN ADVERTISING MESSAGE WORK

As previously mentioned, to make your advertising work it needs
to be seen, read, remembered, believed and acted upon. So how do
you do this? The answer is by conforming to AIDA. This stands
for:

A = Attention
I   = Interest
D = Desire
A = Action

This very simple rule will also make your direct mail letters,
leaflets, brochures and inserts, and e-shots more effective.

ATTENTION

You need to grab the ATTENTION.

You have only a couple of seconds to catch someone's attention before they turn the page, put your mailshot in the waste paper bin, switch off the radio, flick channels on the television, leave the website or press the delete button. So you need to make sure that you grab their attention. To do this you need to be imaginative. Here are some techniques to help you.

Try using a strong headline or a bold question, something that captures or plays on your key benefit. Remember our features and benefits exercise? It is the benefits that persuade people to buy, not the features. One very excellent tool that can help you to analyse the effectiveness of your headlines can be found at www.aminstitute.com, which provides a free online headline analysis.

On television and the internet, you can use a number of techniques to capture the imagination. Television, cinema and the internet use moving pictures with sound and vision – both of which you can exploit – but that doesn't necessarily mean people will keep watching. They may change channels, pop out to make a drink, buy an ice cream, or click off your website if it is too slow to load, therefore missing your expensive advertisement.

Again, you need to think of your target audience. What messages and images would they respond to: humour, horror, shock, romance, cartoons or nostalgia?

You can also use sound effects to grab attention. Loud music, familiar music, contrast in style and levels of music, a catchy jingle, an unusual sound or a good voiceover artist can all work.

In the printed media you can use colour to make your advertisement stand out in a black and white publication. Or you could use a black or coloured border. Borders are very effective. Illustrations or photographs also work well. Or you could use a combination of the above. But **don't** fall into the trap of trying to cram too much text into too small a space. There is some truth in the maxim 'the less said the better', certainly when it comes to advertisements.

Make sure you resist the temptation to over fill your ad- white space is much more effective in drawing the eye.

Q EXAMPLE

James the printer is about to target his existing customers by telling them about a new service his company has just launched. His company is now able to conduct email marketing campaigns. He is designing an advertisement to appear in a regional business magazine, and wants to back this up by a mailing campaign and an email campaign to targeted and selected businesses. He needs to come up with an ATTENTION headline. The feature and benefit of the new service is that James can now provide an email marketing service, which means he can help businesses to target their customers very cost effectively.

His ATTENTION headline could be:

LOOKING TO MAKE THE MOST OF YOUR MARKETING BUDGET?
(this headline scores 22.2% on the online headline analyser)

NOW THERE'S A HIGHLY COST-EFFECTIVE WAY TO REACH MORE BUSINESSES AND GET RESULTS
(this headline scores 42.86% on the headline analyser, so it is a more powerful headline)

NEED A COST-EFFECTIVE WAY TO REACH NEW BUSINESSES?
(this headline scores 66.67% and is by far the most powerful one)

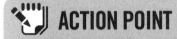

ACTION POINT

- Taking one of your brands or services, write down the key feature and benefit.
- Now define the target audience.
- Next identify the best way of reaching them through advertising (as mentioned in the previous chapter).
- Looking at the key benefit, target audience and the previous section, can you say how you are going to capture their attention?

Keep it simple. Too much text and your advertisement will be lost in all the other text on the page.

Look through the advertisements in magazines and newspapers to see which ones stand

TOP TIPS

Use white space. It will help your advertisement to stand out.

out. Ask yourself why and then adapt the technique to suit your own advertisements.

A mailshot letter or leaflet

In a mailshot letter address the recipient directly, ie Dear Mr Smith, not Dear sir, or Dear householder. You need to create the impression that you are writing to that person as an individual not as a mass mailshot. The more you can personalise your letter or leaflet, the more success you will have. This is where your database using variable data can be a great asset.

A mailshot letter or leaflet should begin with a statement or question, and should contain a key benefit first. In the letter, this is usually presented in bold and goes under the salutation and before the body copy of the letter. So taking one of our previous examples, the opening of the letter would look something like this:

Dear Mr Brown,
NEED A COST-EFFECTIVE WAY TO REACH NEW
BUSINESSES?

Don't begin a mailshot letter with waffle, or with the standard, 'I am writing to introduce my company to you.' It's obvious you are writing, and besides I didn't invite you to introduce your company to me, did I?

If you don't make your letter easy to read then why should your reader bother with it? You haven't got time to wade through lots of text searching for the benefits so don't insult your reader by thinking that he isn't as busy as you are.

INTEREST

Stimulate INTEREST.

Now we need to return to our features and benefits exercise. What are the other benefits you are offering? Make these benefits strong in your advertising copy, mailshot letter and leaflet, to add conviction.

Writing good mailshots

- Use short words, short sentences and short paragraphs.
- Always remember your target audience.
- What language do they speak? What will they respond to?
- Use 'YOU' and 'I' instead of 'WE'.
- Remember you are trying to create the impression of writing to the customer personally so make it user-friendly.
- Use frequent subheadings or bullet points to break up copy.
- Be clear, straightforward, uncluttered and avoid jargon.
- Be as natural as you can, as if you are having a conversation with the person.
- Make it easy to read and don't pad it out with waffle.

Always consider the reader's needs in your advertisement, leaflet, flyer or letter. Make sure you interest him by giving benefits.

TOP TIPS

Remember people always ask, 'What's in it for me?' Address this question in your advertisements, and mailshots. Tell them what's in it for them.

Develop interest with the best benefit you can offer, and win them over with second and further benefits. Follow your copy through from the heading. You must get the reader saying, *'Yes, I must have some of that!'* There must be strong benefits or an offer in the letter or advertisment, tempting the customer where ever he looks.

Make it easy for the reader (or listener if on radio to understand what the offer is. They shouldn't have to spend hours fathoming it out, and of course they won't. To follow on from our previous example let's see how James, our printer, can build on his mailshot letter/leaflet. Here are some further features and benefits of his new email service.

Feature	Which means	Benefit	Therefore
We have partnered with the best marketing agencies in the area	Which means	We are able to provide top-level advice	Helping you to get results
We provide a single point of contact for email marketing, and printed marketing material	Which means	We can help you with your marketing needs whatever the requirement, simply and quickly	Saving you time and hassle

Let's look how we can translate this into copy for our leaflet or mailshot letter.

Dear Mr Brown,

Need a cost effective way to reach new businesses?

Then we can help you. By partnering with some of the best marketing agencies in the area we are able to provide you with a top-level marketing service at affordable prices and from one single point of contact, saving you both valuable time and money.

For many businesses the natural reaction in tough markets is to cut marketing costs – but it is precisely during these difficult times that businesses need to continue to market their products and services in order to win more customers and increase sales.

We can help you achieve results through targeted e-marketing campaigns including newsletters, e-zines, special bulletins and promotions.

Having gained interest you then need to inspire **desire**.

DESIRE

Here you need to strengthen the benefits of your product/service. You can use questions to hold the interest and build desire.

🔍 EXAMPLE

Returning to James, the printer, he can now strengthen his offer with a further benefit:
'What's more, our award-winning design team can make sure your message is communicated in an eye-catching and appropriate style to suit your customers and target customers, generating great results.'

Be enthusiastic. Be friendly. Be helpful.

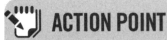

ACTION POINT

Revisit your features and benefits.
Add in the features that would appeal to your target customers and emphasise the benefits of these, for example:
• Free car parking
• A free quotation
• Money-back guarantee
• An accessible location
• Friendly, helpful, expert staff
• Long and convenient opening hours
• An easy way of ordering.
Make your target customers really want what you are offering.

ACTION

Finally, prompt ACTION.

To close, you need a call to action. You could enclose a coupon or a fax-back reply, provide an email and website address – or all four. Tell the customer he can get further information by visiting your website. There you could add a further incentive for the customer to buy from you by including a special offer or discount.

Make it easy for people to respond; let them tick boxes rather than having to fill in forms. Using the variable data from your database you can easily drop their name and address onto the reply form saving them the trouble of filling it in.

Give an incentive for your customers to take action: use a free trial, free consultation, free brochure or possibly a free gift.

Let's look at James, the printer's, complete email.

Dear Mr Brown,

Need a cost effective way to reach new businesses?

Then we can help you. By partnering with some of the best marketing agencies in the area we are able to provide you with a top-level marketing service at affordable prices and from one single point of contact, saving you both valuable time and money.

For many businesses the natural reaction in tough markets is to cut marketing costs – but it is precisely during these difficult times that businesses need to continue to market their products and services in order to win more customers and increase sales.

We can help you achieve results through targeted e-marketing campaigns including newsletters, e-zines, special bulletins and promotions.

What's more our award-winning design team can make sure your message is communicated in an eye-catching and appropriate style to suit your customers and target customers, generating great results.

And if you need printed material to complement your e-marketing messages or to use in a stand-alone campaign, we can also provide a whole range from short print runs, personalised mailshots, brochures and newsletters to producing posters and promotional items.

Our marketing advice can ensure that your budget is spent wisely, and aimed at the correct market, communicating the correct message in the correct way. The initial consultation is completely FREE, so what have you got to lose? Why not call us on 0845 1234 for an informal chat and find out how we can

help your business. Alternatively you can email me at james@
printers.com or visit our website at www.printersrus.com
or complete the reply form and one of our experienced and
helpful staff will contact you.

Yours sincerely,

James Smith
Managing Director

As an advertisement

NEED A COST-EFFECTIVE WAY TO REACH NEW BUSINESSES?

We can make your budgets work harder by providing expert
advice at affordable prices and from one single point of contact.

Get results through targeted e-marketing campaigns, eye-
catching designs and personalised marketing.

Ensure that your budget is spent wisely, and aimed at the
correct market, communicating the correct message in the
correct way.

Call now on 0845 1234 for a FREE consultation and
find out how we can help your business grow.

Visit our website at www.printersrus.com to see our
complete range of services.

Remember AIDA: Attention – Interest – Desire – Action

MORE ABOUT MAILSHOTS

Well-targeted and well-designed mailshots can be an extremely successful form of marketing. They are controllable and the results can be measured. I have already looked at the golden rules for writing mailshot letters and leaflets, but there are some additional rules you'd do well to remember to ensure your mailings don't become junk mail.

Secrets of a good mailshot

The mailing list
This must be as accurate as possible. If you are buying a list, ensure it is from a reputable source and that it has been regularly cleaned. If using your own data, make sure it is as up to date as possible. The mailshot must be targeted to the right person and must be sent to a named individual.

The product/service and the offer
There must be something in the mailshot for the reader – a strong offer and clear benefits.

The sender must have an affinity with the receiver
You need to communicate the right message. In order to be successful you must talk the language of your target customers.

A response mechanism
Make it easy for the reader to respond. Give him a coupon to complete and post, or a fax back or email address. Refer them to your website. Make your telephone number bold to encourage him to pick up the phone to you. In addition, freepost and a free telephone number can help to lift response.

Plan for a campaign

As I have already said, one-off advertisements and mailshots rarely achieve much. Don't bombard people though. Plan a mailshot perhaps once a quarter or three times a year – whichever is relevant and suitable for your products or services, and the industry or consumers you are targeting. You can also use newsletters as a form of mailshot. See Chapter 12 for more information on this and e-newsletters.

QUICK RECAP

- *In order to be effective, advertising must create a sense of familiarity with the target audience.*
- *People buy what they know and recognise.*
- *Advertisements over a period of time raise awareness and build credibility.*
- *The customer must be aware of the brand or company.*
- *There must be some* understanding *of what the product is and what it will do for the customer.*
- *The customer must arrive at the mental* conviction *to buy the product.*
- *The customer must stir himself into* action.
- *Your advertising message should conform to AIDA:*
  A = Attention
  I = Interest
  D = Desire
  A = Action
- *Well-targeted and well-designed mailshots can be an extremely successful form of marketing.*

CHAPTER 11

Email marketing

Using emails to raise the profile of your business or to sell your services or products is a quick, simple and highly cost-effective method of marketing. Emails can be personalised and results can be measured. This chapter examines the dos and don'ts of using email marketing, while the following chapter looks at how to use e-newsletters.

Before you embark on an email marketing campaign, you need to be fully aware of the legislation regarding this form of marketing. Different countries have different legislation on the sending of unsolicited emails, so it is always best to check. A useful website, which can point you in the right direction, is www.marketingtoday. com.

In the UK this legislation is covered by the Privacy in Electronic Communications Directive. The regulations define electronic mail as:

'Any text, voice, sound or image message sent over a public electronic communications network which can be stored in the network or in the recipient's terminal equipment until it is collected by the recipient and includes messages sent using a short message service.'

Messages using Bluetooth technology and sent to all Bluetooth-enabled handsets are also considered to be 'electronic mail'.

In the USA the CAN-SPAM Act of 2003 (Controlling the Assault of Non-Solicited Pornography and Marketing Act) establishes requirements for those who send commercial email, spells out penalties for spammers and companies whose products are advertised in spam if they violate the law, and gives consumers the right to ask emailers to stop spamming them. This website can provide you with the details: www.ftc.gov/bcp/edu/pubs/business/ecommerce/bus61.shtm

IN THE UK

What you can and can't do – part 1

This information applies to business-to-consumer marketing. Individuals are defined as a residential subscriber or a sole trader for a non-limited liability partnership who would use an email address that would look something like the following example: joebloggs@hotmail.com.

In the UK, all email marketing to individuals must be done with their express permission; they must **opt in**.

There is however an exception, which is called the **soft opt in** rule. This is where you can send a marketing email to an individual subscriber without their consent, only if you comply with the following rules:

• You must have obtained the contact details of this person in the course of a sale or negotiation, or in the course of the sale of a product or service

• The marketing information you are sending relates to similar services and products

• The recipient has been given a simple means of refusing the use of his contact details for marketing purposes at the time those details were initially collected

• He did not refuse the use of the details, at the time of each subsequent communication.

If you satisfy these criteria, you do not need prior consent to send marketing by email to individual subscribers.

If collecting emails, or mobile phone numbers, as part of a competition or promotion, make sure you ask the customer if you can use this information to communicate with him in this way on future offers and promotions. If you collect his details and do not make it clear that you would like to contact him by email with further offers in the future, you will breach the regulations.

Buying in or renting a third party list

If you buy in, or rent a list from a third party, you can only use it if it was obtained by that third party on a clear **prior consent** basis, that is where the intended recipient has actively consented to receiving unsolicited emails messages from a third party.

Always seek assurance that the list you are buying or renting has followed the requirements of the law. The third party selling or renting the list must have obtained consent from the customer through the use of a clause. For example, if the third party is a gardening company that subsequently sells or rents its list to other gardening companies then it should have used a clause like the following:

☐ I am happy to hear from other companies that offer gardening products. Please pass my details onto them so that they can contact me.

Or they might have used a clause that is unspecified, for example:

☐ I want to hear from other companies about their online offers. Please pass my details onto them.

However, before emailing the customer you should always check your own database to make sure the person has not already sent an 'opt out' request to you.

> Do not conceal your identity when you contact them and make sure you provide them with a valid contact address for subsequent 'opt outs'.

As with mailshots, the same applies to e-shots in that the older the list, the less likely the recipient is to respond positively to a marketing message, and the more likely you are to waste your time. It might even damage your organisation's reputation if you send poorly targeted marketing messages to individuals who are no longer interested in those services and products.

The best lists are ones that you have built yourself.

What you can and can't do – part 2

This information applies to business-to-business marketing. In the UK you can send a marketing email to those you have on your database without needing to gain their permission first. You must not, however, conceal your identity when you send a marketing message and you must provide a valid address to which the recipient can send an 'opt out' request if he so wishes.

Ask your customers how they prefer to be contacted. This will not only help you to tailor campaigns by sending them the right message in the right way, but will also save you money, and even prevent you from falling foul of the law and incurring penalties. A simple question on correspondence or your website will suffice, for example:

Please contact me by:

☐ Post   ☐ Telephone   ☐ Text   ☐ Email

with further information about your products and services.

Try to aim for permission-based marketing as much as you can, provide a statement of use when you collect details from customers, and put this somewhere visible, so that customers can easily read it. Make it easy for customers to 'opt out' and comply with their requests promptly.

Because people often have more than one email address it might be advisable to include the recipient's email address in the message and a line that says, 'click here to remove xyz@acme. com'. That way the recipient can see which email address is being deleted.

Of course, this regulation does not prevent UK citizens receiving unsolicited email and text messages sent from other countries where the laws are more lenient or non-existent.

You can obtain comprehensive and useful advice about this area of marketing from the website www.ico.gov.uk, or call the Information Commissioner's Office Helpline on 01625 545745.

IN THE USA

In the USA the law requires that your email give recipients an opt-out method. You then have 10 business days to stop sending email to that person's address. It is also illegal to sell or transfer the email addresses of people who choose not to receive your email, even in the form of a mailing list.

TOP TIPS

- Make sure that all your staff capture email addresses.
- They should ask permission to contact the prospect or customer by email.
- Consider running a telemarketing campaign to build an email list, or a direct marketing campaign to capture email addresses.
- Refer customers to your website where they can register for updates or your e-newsletter, or obtain free information (see Chapter 12 on e-newsletters).
- Offer an incentive that you can fulfil electronically, for example a free report or fact sheet that can be downloaded from your website.
- Keep the data clean.
- Personalise messages so you avoid them looking and sounding like spam.
- Don't bombard people with messages. Once a month or every six weeks is enough.

DOES EMAIL MARKETING WORK?

Is it worth it? After reading the above, I wouldn't blame you if you were thinking should I bother? Does email marketing work, especially given the amount that we all have to cope with today, and the spam that we continually receive? Well, the quick answer to that is yes, it can work, but I am acutely aware that anything that concerns the internet and technology can be relevant one day and practically extinct the next.

The way, therefore, to make your marketing more effective is not just to consider one method of reaching your customers, but several. And, of course, you will not be sending them email marketing messages if they do not wish to receive them.

Your campaigns might consist of telemarketing the customer or prospective customer, sending direct mail and following up with electronic mail. Or it might be sending an email and then following up with a letter, or phone call.

BENEFITS OF AN EMAIL CAMPAIGN

The major benefits of an email campaign are:
- It is quick, simple and highly cost effective
- It can be personalised
- Click-throughs can be tracked and responses measured
- The ability to click on a link to a website is a great asset.

MORE EFFECTIVE EMAIL MARKETING

Build a list

In-house lists usually generate the best response, so build a list of your customers, both existing and new. If you don't have their email addresses then you might wish to run a telemarketing campaign to capture them, but ensure you explain exactly why you want the email address, and how you will be using it. If the customer doesn't wish to give you permission to contact him with promotional offers by email then he has the right to do so.

Write appealing email copy

Subject heading
You have about three seconds to get the recipient's attention before he decides to read it or delete it. Be short and to the point, give him a reason to open the mail, grab his attention, but don't make it too gimmicky or it could look like spam. It should be clear from the subject header what the email is about. Think about your offer and your target customers, also your key benefit. Subject lines should be no more than about five to eight words.

The only time you might expand on this is for a news release to the media, or as the subject header for your e-newsletter.

Think of the subject line as one sentence that **TOP TIPS** can summarise your campaign.

Not easy I know, but essential. Be clear and concise.

Q EXAMPLE

Taking our previous example of James the printer, the email subject header could be:
A cost-effective way to reach new businesses

Make it chatty

Emails are more natural in their style of communication than formal letters. Make it chatty, in the right tone of voice to suit your target audience. Read it aloud: how does it sound? The email must sound personal to that customer, even though you are targeting many. Check your spelling, punctuation and grammar.

Use language that communicates directly on a one-to-one basis; don't let it look like spam. Don't use the word 'free', or use lots of capitals and exclamation marks – it will look tacky. If you can, personalise it with the information you have about that customer or group of customers.

Keep it brief

Once again, you are trying to satisfy that basic question the customer is asking himself, ie 'What's in it for me?' Why should the recipient read the email and why would he be interested in what you have to offer?

The first couple of lines are critical. Short simple sentences and clarity is vital.

Like the direct mail letter it will be scanned before it is read properly, so you have only a short space of time to capture and hold the reader's attention.

Lead your customers to your website for further benefits and details of how to contact you. A simple landing page will give you extra space for you to convince them.

THINGS TO AVOID

Don't try to do it all in one hit
Like most other forms of marketing, it takes time to build awareness and communicate a message. Remember, your messages need to be seen, read, remembered, believed and then acted upon.

Email marketing is not a one-hit wonder; think of it as a long-term communicating process.

Don't type the email address in the 'To' field
This means that your recipients can see all your mailing addresses. It destroys the illusion that you are communicating only with that person as an individual, it looks totally unprofessional and it breaks a confidence. It leaves the individuals on the list open to being contacted by everyone else. If you are using Outlook or Outlook Express then put your own email address in the 'To' field, and use the 'BCC' (Blind Carbon Copy) field for your mailing address emails. This way it will keep your list safely hidden from the other recipients.

Don't send your main message as an attachment
This will reduce your chances of the email message being read because many people are rightly scared of opening attachments because of the dangers of viruses.

BULK MAILERS

You can use Outlook and Outlook Express to send your mailings, but once your mailing list gets to a certain size you will probably find this an inefficient way of doing it. When sending large mailings, your internet service provider (ISP) might think you're a spammer and therefore suspend your service, and you will also receive a higher number of bounce-backs. If you are using Outlook or Outlook Express then limit the number of people you are copying in (using BCC) to a maximum of about 10 per email.

There are companies that will help you to set up an emailing service, provide readymade HTML templates for you to drop in your own logo, colours and text, and some can provide tracking information on who and how many people opened your email, and how many clicked through to your website. Alternatively you can buy bulk mailing software and create your own templates and email lists using this.

Your web developer might also be able to help by setting up a system using your website to send out your promotional mailings.

TEST IT

Come up with a couple of different styles of email messages and send them as test messages either back to yourself to see what they look like in your inbox, or to a number of people in your company, or even to one or two 'tame' customers. Test it on a small sample of people, and if it works roll it out.

No matter how many times you check an email, or test it, though, you might still find that some error has slipped through. Unless it is a critical error, for example the incorrect price, incorrect date or essential missing information, it is best to leave it. Sending out another email correcting the error can be a waste of time, look unprofessional and also draws people's attention to an error they didn't even notice in the first place!

> The most successful email campaigns are those that build on responses. Like all marketing, people buy what they are familiar with, so keep it going.

QUICK RECAP

- *Check the legislation in the country you are targeting before embarking on a campaign.*
- *If you buy or rent a list from a third party, you can only use it if it was obtained by that third party on a clear **prior consent** basis.*
- *Do not conceal your identity when you contact the customer by email.*
- *Provide a valid contact address for subsequent 'opt outs'.*
- *The older the list, the less likely the recipient is to respond positively to a marketing message.*
- *The best lists are ones that you build yourself.*
- *Keep the data clean, and personalise messages.*
- *Ask your customers how they prefer to be contacted.*
- *Provide a statement of use when you collect details and put this somewhere visible, so that customers can easily read it.*
- *When writing email copy, be short and to the point, give the recipient a reason to open the mail.*
- *Use language that communicates directly on a one-to-one basis; don't let it look like spam.*
- *Lead your customers to your website for further details and benefits.*
- *Test it.*

CHAPTER 12

Newsletters, e-newsletters and corporate brochures

Regular and content-specific newsletters are a very effective marketing tool, whether that is the printed or the e-newsletter version. Newsletters can keep your existing customers and target customers informed of new products and services, and they help to keep your company name in front of your customers on a regular basis. They build credibility and engender a feeling of trust. This chapter examines how to make your newsletters, e-newsletters and corporate brochures more effective.

NEWSLETTERS AND E-NEWSLETTERS

> In order to work, newsletters must be produced regularly.

Newsletters are not an easy option. They take time and effort to produce and it also takes you a while to build a good subscriber base.

> The first step in launching a successful newsletter is to be clear about your objectives. You will also need to know your target audience.

Only then can you provide information your customers and prospective customers want and value. If your customers are extremely diverse then you should consider developing more than one newsletter or e-newsletter and tailoring the information to suit that particular group of customers. Alternatively, you could tailor the front and back pages, but keep the content inside the newsletter the same for each group of customers. Not that your newsletter has to be four pages; it can easily be a two-page double-sided affair.

Subscribers/mailing list
Your existing customers are the obvious starting point for subscribers to your newsletter, but you will also be keen to add new prospects to this list, to build a dialogue with them over time and boost your chances of winning new business from them.

 ACTION POINT

- Examine your target customers and decide which groups would benefit from a newsletter. Are you looking at producing one newsletter or tailoring it to suit the different groups?
- Which groups would respond well to an email newsletter, and which would prefer a printed version?
- Say how often you think you would be able to send a newsletter.

Building a subscription list

• Position subscription details on your website.

• Offer an incentive for your customers to subscribe, eg a free guide or information.

• Make sure that information about your newsletters and e-newsletters are in your company brochures and leaflets, along with information telling the customer how he can subscribe.

• Send a press release to your local, regional and trade press, launching the-newsletter or e-newsletter.

• Add in the launch issue some useful advice that potential subscribers need.

• Invite a subscription with every email you send linked into your signature, and add the link to your website.

• Remind subscribers to forward the e-newsletter to their contacts or friends and so help to spread the word (viral marketing).

• Make sure that everyone in your company knows about the-newsletter and/or e-newsletter and encourage them to tell new and prospective customers about it.

Content is critical

Newsletters and e-newsletters are **not** company puff and they are **not** the hard sell. They must have information of real value to the subscriber. You also need to make your newsletter stand out from others. You want your subscribers to look forward to receiving the newsletter. At least 80% of the information should be meaty content written in an editorial style.

> Give them news, information and advice; not what you think you should sell them.

Put yourself in the shoes of your target customers and think about what they would like to read. Content can include interviews, case studies, snippets of news, fun articles, FAQs. What is the personality of your organisation? Reflect that in your newsletter.

Consistency and timing

Developing a personality for your newsletter will help it stand out from the competition. Consistency is also critical. Make sure you draw up a publication timetable and stick to it – no excuses that you were too busy to bring out the summer edition. If you skip an issue your customers/subscribers will feel they can no longer rely on you, and you also break that loyalty chain you are trying to forge. The frequency with which you issue your newsletter depends on how much you have to say and your target audience. E-newsletters tend to come out with more frequency than the printed version. You may wish to issue an e-newsletter once a month, and a printed version once a quarter. You don't have to issue both, either is effective on its own. However, whatever you decide, be realistic about whether or not it is achievable for you. Don't promise something you can't deliver.

Customer feedback

 ACTION POINT

Examine your emailing contacts and group these into different types of customer with the same characteristics. For example, you can build distinct lists with customers from the same type of industry; your existing customers could be another email list; and target customers another.

Now think about what kind of content each grouping would like to receive from you.
• Do you need to send different e-newsletters to these groups?
• How frequently do you need to produce a newsletter or e-newsletter?

Draw up a timetable, and make someone in your organisation responsible for making it happen.

Encourage customer feedback. This can be done through a competition or invite them to post a comment or join a forum on your website.

Develop a questionnaire to get feedback on your organisation's products or services. Send this out with your newsletter, or put a link to your website on your e-newsletter. Offer to enter responses into a free prize draw, or provide a discount or a money-off voucher for their next purchase.

CORPORATE BROCHURES

Do you need a corporate brochure? What are you going to do with it when you get it? I have been to many organisations where the corporate brochure has cost the earth and yet it sits in the bottom of a cupboard collecting dust. I have even had people say to me that their brochure is too expensive for them to send out – what was the point of producing it then! Here are some questions and tips to help you decide if you need a corporate brochure and how you are going to use it.

Considerations for a corporate brochure
- Is it to be mailed to people on request?
- Is it to be displayed in reception?
- Is it to be taken to an exhibition or is it for use by the sales force?
- Is it to be used as a mailout? If so, would you be better off producing a mailing leaflet rather than a corporate brochure?
- Who is your brochure aimed at?
- Do you need several brochures to communicate with each group of customers?
- What special, unique selling points or benefits are you going to emphasise in your brochure? What corporate image are you trying to portray?
- What is the personality of your company and how can this be communicated in your brochure?

- Does the brochure need photographs or illustrations?
- Should it be full colour, one colour or two?
- What size should it be?

In addition, try not to have too many people involved in the design of a corporate brochure, because they will all have different views about what they like. The end result can be something that looks as though it's been designed by a committee, and the essential message and image will have been diluted, or even lost completely. Remember it is not what *you* would like in a brochure, but what your target audience would like.

And, of course, look at your budget. Corporate brochures can be expensive.

Make sure you spend your money wisely, on a brochure that serves its purpose, and one that will work for you and reach the right target audience.

Writing the corporate brochure

When writing content for a corporate brochure, you will need to decide what essential information should be included. Does it have to explain the complete range of products or services or only some of them?

As an alternative to the corporate brochure (or perhaps in conjunction with it) you might consider producing a corporate DVD. Again, you need to consider your target

TOP TIPS Remember to stress benefits and write it in a style that your customers will respond to.

audience: is this something they would be receptive towards? How can your company and its image, its products or services, be communicated via a DVD? Is it the best vehicle for your message? Also consider budgets.

If you produce a catalogue, could you put this on a CD rather than having a printed version? Do you need both? Always consider your target audience and how they would respond to and use a brochure.

You might consider making your brochure available as a download through your website, or perhaps from a page that can be easily printed. Your brochure should reflect the style and design of your website.

QUICK RECAP

- *Newsletters are a very effective marketing tool: they can keep both your existing customers and target customers informed of new products and services.*
- *They help to keep your company name in front of your customers on a regular basis.*
- *They build credibility and engender a feeling of trust.*
- *Be clear about your objectives and know your target audience.*
- *Remind subscribers to forward your e-newsletter to their contacts or friends.*
- *Newsletters should contain information of value.*
- *Draw up a publication timetable and stick to it.*
- *Include a questionnaire to get customer feedback on your products/services.*
- *Decide if you need a corporate brochure and how you are going to use it.*
- *Don't have too many people involved in the design of a corporate brochure, because they will all have different views about what they like.*
- *Stress the **benefits** and write it the style your customers will respond to.*
- *Consider making your brochure available as a download through your website.*

CHAPTER 13

Websites, blogs and viral marketing

Your website can be many things: a shop window, a corporate brochure, a meeting place, an advice centre, a shop and much, much more. It needs to reflect your company's image and products, and it must be designed with your customers in mind. This chapter explores the issues of successful website marketing.

The days when companies had to decide whether or not to have a website have long since past; for any organisation today a website is a must. Over the years websites have evolved. To begin with all that was required was a presence, something that your customers could click through from the address on a brochure or advertisement. The next stage of website development saw designs becoming flashier and more complex with moving images and gadgets. Some are still like this today. That's all very well and they certainly look impressive, but nobody will visit them if they can't find them in search engines such as Google and Yahoo!, and if customers can't access them and use them quickly.

> It's not a bit of good having an award-winning-stunningly designed website if no one can find it.

Today, your website needs to be a place where your customers and target customers can have a dialogue with you, as well as gain further information about your products or services. They should be able to get a feel for your organisation, buy your products if appropriate, or enquire further about your services. Your website needs to be seen and found by the search engines, and that means having a site that has been developed and designed by an experienced website developer rather than a traditional graphic designer. But the first rule of marketing still applies:

> Remember your customers and make your website attractive to them.

WEBSITE DESIGN

What kind of structure do you need?

Firstly, your website should be easy to read. The text should not be too small that your customers can't see it, or too large so the site screams at them. Most text should be left aligned and only the headlines should be centred. Limit the graphics, or ensure they fit with the content of the website. One of the most important aspects of website design, apart from making it attractive to your target customers, is clean and easy navigation and keeping the vital information **above the fold**, which is what your customers immediately see on the screen without having to scroll down. If you are selling products, or have a special offer, then it would be advisable to display it 'above the fold'. Put longer content further down the page.

TOP TIPS

Make sure your website is quick to download. Research has shown that if it doesn't download within 15 seconds, visitors will move on.

Have a clean and logical hierarchy to your site, and a good page structure so that it is easy for your customers to find what they are seeking. When people use the internet they are looking for instant access to information and would rather click off your site and visit another if what they are searching for isn't within easy reach.

Navigation is generally found along the top of your website or on the left hand side – or both if the design of your site allows it, though this isn't always possible. All of your hyperlinks should be clear to the visitor. These are usually in a different colour, different size font or both.

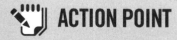

ACTION POINT

Examine your existing website.
• How quick did it download?
• Could the navigation be improved?
• Is critical information 'above the fold'?

Personality

Your website and its content should reflect the personality of your organisation, so revisit what your organisation stands for. Are you trying to portray a fun and friendly image like the Marmite website I mentioned earlier, or is your business or its products or services more serious? Look at the key benefits or unique selling points of your products and services, you will need to bring these into your website content and possibly the design.

Who forms your target audience? Are they adults or children? What is their lifestyle, their background? What type of language and design would they respond to?

What are you trying to achieve through your website? Are you aiming for online sales? Do you want people to make enquiries? Are you seeking feedback on your services or products?

Be clear from the start about the purpose of your website.

Do you need to provide a secure, online buying service? Or would a simple enquiry or 'contact us' form suffice for your organisation?

Do you need an online forum where your customers can meet other like-minded customers, or post comments on your services or products?

Content

Write concisely, preferably using no more than 12 words per line, as users don't want to read reams of text online. Research has shown that people tend to scan text on screen. It is also harder for many people to read from a computer screen than it is from paper.

If you're trying desperately to attract the attention of the search engines then what you write might not make any sense to your target customer.

Return to the chapter on writing advertising copy; your website content needs to act in

TOP TIPS

Write as you speak, and write for your target audience, not with the search engine in mind.

the same way. A good strong headline to draw people in; lots of interesting content and benefits to keep them there; and a call to action to make them respond. Give them a compelling reason to stay. Make the right impression. Use graphics but not too many that it confuses the message.

Your contact information should be easy to find.

You can use a 'contact us' form on your website, but have one designed where the customer can add a code to the contact form before being allowed to submit it – this will help to eliminate spammers. You can also give names and email contacts (although some spammers will trawl for these) or provide a telephone number and contact mailing address.

Add an RSS feed to the bottom of each page so that visitors can subscribe to your website and easily pick up the latest news. An RSS (Rich Site Summary) is a format for delivering regularly changing web content. Many news-related sites, weblogs and other online publishers syndicate their content as an RSS feed to whoever wants it, at no charge.

The headings

This is important in two ways: one, it does the critical job of drawing your reader in and making them want to read further; two, it will be picked up by the search engines. As previously mentioned, one way of analysing the power of your headlines is to use the free headline analysing tool at www.aminstitute.com. See if what you've come up with is powerful and emotive enough for your target audience.

ANALYSING AND TRACKING YOUR WEBSITE

Ensure that you can measure the results of your website, to analyse how people use it and what keywords they use to find you, where they are coming from and how long they stay on a page and on your website. Google Optimizer can help you test various pages, design, content and keywords to get the best results, and Google Analytics can tell you how people found your site, the search terms they used and whether they converted to customers. Stat Counter is another very useful tracking and analytical tool and is free up to a certain number of hits. It is easy to bolt on to a website or blog and can provide you with useful information. You can find more details on Google Analytics and Stat Counter by doing a search on the internet.

TOP TIPS

- Keep sentences short.
- Use bullet points or numbered lists where possible and keep page length short.
- Use highlighted links to take your visitor to further information.
- Use plenty of headings, subheadings and white space, which makes it easier to read.
- Avoid centring text and don't use all capitals.
- Avoid excessive italics; use them for emphasis only.
- Check the colours you use aren't bad for those with various forms of colour blindness; if in doubt make it black and white and see if it still makes sense.
- Navigation should be as easy as possible: either on the left hand side of the page or across the top. It should take up as little space as possible. Keep it in the same consistent style across the website.
- Put your logo and other corporate statements in the same place across the website.
- Use graphics sparingly as they add to the download time. Keep the file as small as possible.
- Test your website on various browsers and window sizes.

GENERATING TRAFFIC TO YOUR WEBSITE

Search engine optimisation (SEO) and link building are crucial to a successful website. It's all very well having a website but not much use if nobody visits it. First, make sure that you have all the obvious areas covered, such as your web address on every piece of marketing material and stationery available for your business. If you are writing an article for a publication, make sure to include your web address in it or at the end of it so that people can visit it for further information.

> You need your website to be seen and registered by search engines.

Some businesses use specialist consultants for this area. These are called search engine optimisation consultants; and as in all walks of life, there are good ones and bad ones, so before you part with any money, check out their credentials. They should ideally have a marketing background and will want to understand your business and its objectives before offering any solutions. There is, however, a great deal you can do yourself to make sure that your website is recognised by the search engines.

Keywords

When deciding which keywords are critical for your website and for visitors to find you, a good starting point is with your features and benefits exercise, which we looked at in Chapter 2. What are your products or services? Make a list of them and the key benefits they offer. Now you have a logical route to finding your keywords. They must also be words and phrases that will be regularly searched for.

Q EXAMPLE

I write a blog about my crime novels. The detective in my marine mystery crime novels sails and lives on his boat, which in the first three books, is a Winkle Brig. *I put this word on my blog and using Stat Counter to monitor visitors and analyse traffic found that hits on my blog increased by 200%. I hadn't realised that* Winkle Brig *sailing boats were so popular. This had the affect of increasing traffic to my site but possibly not increasing sales of my crime novels, because those searching for Winkle Brigs might not necessarily buy crime novels. If my objective here had been to raise my profile, then to a degree I succeeded. If it was to boost sales of my books then I was not so successful.*

Keyword selection is often a process of trial and error. It will need to be constantly monitored, updated and changed.

You need to choose words and phrases that are regularly searched on. Taking my example above, I need to include 'crime novel', 'crime novels', and 'thrillers' as well as 'marine mystery' and 'marine mysteries'. If there are different spellings in different countries for your products you should perhaps include 'tires' and 'tyres' or 'centre' and 'center'. Be aware of all these permutations.

There are a number of keyword finders on the market and software available, including Adwords keyword finder and Stat Counter.

Headings

These are used to emphasise or introduce new topics. Headings come in various sizes represented by tags such as <H1>, <H2>, <H3>, etc. Some of the search engines give extra relevance to keywords that appear within a heading tag – particularly <H1> and <H2> tags, so try to use your important keyword phrase in one or two heading tags on each page.

Link text

The text within a **link** is sometimes weighed more heavily than words found in the regular body text. So again, see if you can use your keywords in a link to either another website or to a page on your own website, or use it either side of the actual link. For example, 'click here to read more about successful marketing techniques' (then insert your webpage link).

Images and videos

Google is integrating images into its main search results as well as its stand-alone image search. Be sure to optimise any images that you have on your website, particularly product images by giving the image a relevant file name when you upload it to your site and not just calling it 'image1.jpg'. For example, if the image is of the front cover of this book then it should be labelled 'Successful Marketing' not 'bookimage1.jpg'. In addition, use a description around the image using the keywords where possible. For example, 'business book on marketing techniques and strategies'. And if you have videos on your website, then make sure you submit them to Google Video as video results are integrated into Google's main search results. Don't forget to submit videos to YouTube at the same time (also owned by Google).

Other tools

There are a number of other tools on Google (all free) that could help your website feature higher in the search engines. These include Google Product Search where, if you have an e-commerce site, you can submit your products to Google, all completely free, and Google will list them in search results in the product search. There is also Google Maps. Again you can register for free and you may well find your business ranking in the Google Maps results which often appear at the top of the search results. It's a great way to get found and can really increase the visibility of your website. For all the tools that are available through Google visit www.google.co.uk /options.

Building links

Building links is another and very highly effective way of getting higher in the search engine rankings.

> The more links you have on other websites, the higher you are rated.

Search engines like Google look for quality links pointing to websites and these links can drive targeted traffic. The more quality links you have, the higher you will appear in the search engines which means your target customers can find you. But building links takes time and effort.

> You can start by considering which sites you'd like to be linked with.

Your suppliers might be an obvious starting point. Then there are other organisations with which you do business, or perhaps you're a member of a business organisation or trade body and can have links from its site. Are there any sites that complement yours? Conduct searches to see which sites might provide a good link. There are also web directories such as The Open Directory and Yahoo!.

 ACTION POINT

- Make a list of the sites you want to contact.
- Are any of the links paid (sometimes this happens) and if so, how much do you have to pay for the link?
- Keep a record of the date you submitted your site and to whom, so you don't lose track of it and can chase if necessary.
- Prepare some text that you can give to a partnering site to use to link to your website. Don't rely on the partnering site to write your text link for you. Make sure your link text contains appropriate keywords and is an objective description.
- Plan for ongoing searches to find new websites to partner with.

If your products are reviewed online then there will be a link from your product to your site, increasing your links and again helping you to build credibility and climb the search engine ranking.

Depending on your product or service, you might develop a following amongst your customers for your products, and they in turn might have their own blogs and websites or presence on social networking sites. You could join a social networking site and put a link between your profile on this and your site. This is known as **viral marketing**, where you are spreading the word about your products or services through the internet.

You might also consider joining affiliate programmes to advertise other companies' products and services on your website and therefore not only generate traffic to your site but earn revenue. You get paid whenever a visitor or your site clicks through to the affiliate's website and makes a purchase.

Give someone in your team the responsibility for looking after your website and ensuring that content is kept fresh.

TOP TIPS Make sure that your website can be easily updated, preferably by you or by a member of your staff.

BLOGS

When launching a new website, it can take some time for it to be recognised by search engines – often six months to a year. It will also take you time to build links. So one way you might consider generating interest and traffic to your website in the meantime could be to begin a blog.

A blog was originally defined as an online diary, but has become so much more than this. In reality it is a website, and what's more it is free and easy to use. If you start a blog using Google, then it will immediately be recognised, and on this blog you can provide a link to your website for more information. But a word of caution: don't use your blog blatantly as a selling tool;

it needs to provide interesting and informative content, which also needs to be updated regularly. This doesn't mean once every six months; it means you will need to write something fresh for your blog at least once a week. Perhaps you can use it to give free advice to clients, or as a blow-by-blow account of how you started your business, or the world of work in which you operate. Check out some existing blogs to see how they are used. As with all internet-based communications, though, consider carefully what you are saying because once it's out there, it stays out there and you don't want any damaging remarks returning to haunt you.

You might also wish to consider having a blog on your organisation's website. Search engines love fresh content and a blog with up-to-date news and snippets of information will be picked up and will help to push you nearer the top of the search engine ranking.

VIRAL MARKETING

This is a term used to increase brand awareness or word of mouth through the internet. It uses pre-existing social networks to spread 'word of mouth' online. It can also use blogs to spread the word.

If people find your blog interesting enough – whether this is a blog on your website or a separate one – then they will flag it up to follow it. They may also mention it on their own blog and provide a link; all of which serves to spread the word about you, your services, product or organisation.

Viral marketing means that people will pass on and share interesting or funny content and so create an awareness and even demand for the product or brand. YouTube videos are shared by many people and can be imported onto websites and social network pages and groups which exist on Facebook, MySpace, Bebo and others.

Often the goal of viral marketing is to generate media coverage via offbeat stories.

Viral marketing is a huge growth area with the popularity of social networks growing at a phenomenal rate. With the average Briton now spending 164 minutes on the internet every day, (according to Google), it should come as no surprise that influence through word of mouth in the digital arena is critical to an organisation.

The film and music industry has already harnessed the power of the internet by tapping into and utilising online opinion formers. Now, when planning a marketing, advertising or promotional campaign, it is simply not enough to think only in terms of the printed and tangible matter: these campaigns need to include and embrace online marketing.

From blogs to social networks, the internet is not just a tool for the young; all ages access and use it. When a campaign takes off, it can gather a momentum that can ripple across sales in all channels. The internet can be buzzing with it.

Q EXAMPLE

Hotmail used viral marketing by adding the line 'Get your free email at Hotmail' to the end of outgoing emails and this way recruited 12 million new subscribers. In 2004, when Google repeated the trick with Gmail by allowing 1,000 opinion formers to 'invite friends', they created three million signups within three months.

OTHER WAYS TO GENERATE TRAFFIC

You could consider generating traffic instantly by taking out advertising with pay-per-click campaigns with Google Adwords or Yahoo! Search Marketing and Microsoft AdCenters. You can set your budgets without worrying about overspending but keep a careful check on this.

You can launch your website, or stimulate traffic to it, with email marketing campaigns as mentioned earlier in this book. Or consider writing online articles for websites, or offer to be a guest blogger on those sites your customers would visit. Also consider making a short video or podcast about your company, services or products. You can post these on YouTube, your website and on social network sites.

QUICK RECAP

- *Identify which unique selling points or benefits you are going to emphasise on your website. These can help you identify keywords.*
- *When designing and writing your website, remember your target audience.*
- *Make your website quick and easy to use, have a clean and logical hierarchy to your site and good page structure.*
- *Keep important information **above the fold**.*
- *Use links to take your visitor to further information.*
- *Use plenty of headings, subheadings and white space, which makes it easier to read.*
- *Use graphics sparingly as they add to the download time.*
- *Test your site on various browsers and window sizes.*
- *Consider starting a blog or adding one to your website, and remember to update it frequently: search engines love fresh content.*
- *Update your website regularly.*
- *Plan how to build links to other websites to increase your search engine ranking.*

CHAPTER 14

Exhibitions

Exhibitions and trade fairs can be a very good way
of generating leads and meeting exciting customers,
but they can also be highly time consuming and very
expensive. In this chapter I examine how to make
them work for you.

Before agreeing to undertake an exhibition you should ask yourself why you are exhibiting. What do you hope to achieve from it?

Here are some objectives for exhibiting:

- To meet existing customers and improve your relationship with them.
- To meet potential customers, identify new opportunities and prepare the ground for future sales.
- To promote your organisation and its image.
- To inform customers and potential customers of new services/ products or changes.
- To obtain sales leads.
- To keep your organisation's name and profile in front of your customers and potential customers.

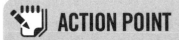 **ACTION POINT**

Ask yourself the following questions before deciding to exhibit:

- Is it the right exhibition for my business?
- Are my customers and potential customers going to be there?
- Who will be attending the exhibition?
- How are the organisers promoting the exhibition?
- Are they going to do enough to attract visitors?
- What will it cost me?
- Cost of the space
  - Cost of hiring or producing a stand
  - Cost of material
  - Cost of your time
  - Cost of any lost business whilst I, or my staff, are away.

THE EXHIBITION STAND

This is often a shell, three panels, two either side and a back drop, which you will need to personalise with promotional material about your organisation. Alternatively, you might consider having your own custom-made stand designed and built. You will also need to take into consideration the furniture you require for that stand. You'll need somewhere for your staff and customers to sit and a table for leaflets and for writing on. The exhibition organisers usually rent out furniture. This can come inclusive in the price of the stand space or you may have to pay extra. All this needs to be taken into consideration when budgeting for an exhibition or trade fair, so make sure that you are clear from the outset what is provided in the cost of booking space.

You'll also need to decide who is going to design your stand and what design and message you want that stand to communicate. Think about the image you wish to create and what you are promoting at this exhibition.

Your stand should be welcoming and accessible.

Corner stands are ideal as access is available from three directions. Alternatively, a stand sited at the bottom of a stairwell can prove to be a good location. Be careful of stands located near the bar as you may find an overspill of drinkers near you, which could put off genuine visitors. They might also block visibility of your stand.

TOP TIPS

You should market the fact that you will be attending an exhibition or trade fair well in advance. This will help to generate more visitors to your stand during the exhibition.

BEFORE THE EXHIBITION

Send out a press release to the relevant media, but don't forget to make it interesting. It's not enough to tell the media you will be at an exhibition. Add something special to spice it up, for example, are you launching a new product or service? Are you going to be running an exciting and high-value competition? Are you offering something free for the first dozen visitors? Or perhaps include an exclusive interview with a personality, celebrity or a well-known respected guru in your particular industry. Post something on your website or create a special webpage to promote this and to give website visitors further information. Perhaps you could offer an incentive for them to contact you to arrange an appointment for the exhibition.

TOP TIPS

To maximise the opportunities at the exhibition, try to arrange as many appointments as you can beforehand with your customers and prospects.

Encourage your customers to visit your stand. This gives you a good opportunity to discuss your services or products on neutral territory.

Conduct a mailing campaign to tell your target audience about your presence at the exhibition, send out a mailshot and/or an e-shot, or conduct a mobile marketing campaign sending text messages to your targets. Take some advertising in the relevant trade or consumer publications.

Offer an incentive for visitors to your stand. Or arrange an on-stand demonstration, if appropriate to your business, and invite them to attend at a certain time.

Most exhibitions and trade fairs have a dedicated website where you could post a press release or take advertising space.

LITERATURE

Make sure you have the right literature – and don't display it too neatly otherwise visitors will be afraid of disturbing your work of art.

It is also a good idea to have something moving on display and I don't mean the staff! A piece of equipment, a computer programme, or a DVD can be ideal. If played loudly, it attracts visitors to your stand. But make sure it doesn't run on endlessly. Stop and start it at loud places especially when visitors to your stand are flagging.

STAFFING

Ensure you have enough staff on your stand. You should always have at least two people on the stand for the majority of time. Exhibition work is very tiring and people do need to take a break, to have a coffee and go to the toilet. In addition, if you have at least two people, there can be a pre-arranged signal between them to get rid of the time wasters.

AT THE EXHIBITION

- Don't just sit there – stand. This encourages people to come on to your stand.
- Don't guard the entrance with your arms folded across your chest and your legs planted apart – you will look like a police officer.
- Avoid negative body language signals.
- Smile at people and talk to them.
- People are wary and reluctant to open conversations, so ensure you do it.
- Open the conversation gently; talk about something neutral, for example the weather.
- Use 'open' questions to get information. Open questions begin with, 'who', 'what', 'where', 'when', 'how', and 'why'.
- If interest is expressed, make sure you get the visitor's contact details.
- Give them your literature, or business card.

157

- Run a promotion encouraging people to give you their details for your database or to encourage them to buy.
- Don't have alcohol on your stand – it only encourages the loafers, time wasters and drunks! But do have coffee, water or orange juice etc.
- Visit the other exhibitors and try to do some business, make contacts.

AFTER THE EXHIBITION

Many organisations fail to track the results of an exhibition. This seems crazy when you think of the amount of money they cost. You must evaluate the success or otherwise of undertaking that exhibition and you must be prepared to track contacts for some time afterwards; months, years even. Look at:

- How many leads you generated?
- How many orders you gained?
- Ask if the exhibition was worth attending and would you do it again.
- How much did it cost you – was this recovered with orders received?

Ruthlessly follow up all contacts made, and keep in touch with them. Use mailshots, e-shots, telephone calls and newsletters to do so.

QUICK RECAP

- *Why are you exhibiting? Be clear on what you hope to gain from attending.*
- *Ask yourself if it is the right exhibition for your business.*
- *How are the organisers promoting the exhibition?*
- *What will it cost?*
- *Who is responsible for the design of your stand?*
- *Have at least two people on the stand for the majority of time.*
- *Track the results of an exhibition.*
- *Ruthlessly follow up all contacts made, and keep in touch with them.*

CHAPTER 15

Sponsorship and sales promotion

Sponsoring an event or an individual, or working with a charity can be an effective way of communicating your message to your target group of customers, and can give you exposure to new groups of potential customers. Sales promotion techniques can help to boost an ailing product or launch a new one or stimulate sales. This chapter examines how to make your sponsorship more successful and the various pros and cons of sale promotion techniques.

SPONSORSHIP

Sponsorship can help to position you in the marketplace and raise your organisation's profile. However, care needs to be taken when choosing who or what to sponsor, because you do not wish to run the risk of portraying a negative image. Decide first what you hope to achieve through sponsorship, ie why are you doing it?

If it's just the case of buying the local football or cricket team their kit because your son or daughter happens to play for them, then that's fine; but that's not really sponsorship in its truest sense, it's more of a charitable donation. So, think about your objectives. Your objectives could be:

• To enhance the image or reputation of your organisation.
• To build links in the community.
• To reach a new target audience.
• To promote your company name and image.

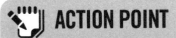 **ACTION POINT**

Questions to ask around sponsorship

• How will the target group see your company name?
• In what connection will it be associated?
• Where will it be advertised?
• How much will you have to pay for the sponsorship and what does this cover?
• What can you get out of it? For example, additional press coverage.
• What else is running around the time of the sponsorship that you could capitalise on? For example, could you run a competition?
• Also consider the extra costs of sponsorship, eg press coverage, events, competitions etc.
• Are there any other sponsors? Are they your competitors?
• How long will the sponsorship last?

Maximising your sponsorship takes time, effort and additional costs over and above what you are paying for the sponsorship; so make sure you have the resources to do it and the commitment to make it work.

It doesn't have to be a big sponsorship deal such as the Olympics or the London Marathon; many successful sponsorship deals can be forged between local companies and charities, and other organisations.

Decide if you are going to organise any corporate hospitality around the event.

Q EXAMPLE

A firm of accountants decided to sponsor an art exhibition by students of the local art college rather than buying off-the-shelf prints for their new office premises. This helped to provide them with some new contacts in the community, and to raise their profile in an interesting and innovative way. In addition, it gave them some lively and unique images for their premises. To capitalise on this sponsorship the senior partner of the accountancy firm became one of the judges and he invited a couple of his key clients and the head of the art department at the local college to be the other judges. The accountancy firm held a drinks reception and invited its clients and some prospective clients to the awards ceremony. A link from the accountancy firm's website to the college's website was established and after the awards ceremony, a special webpage was created and hosted on both organisations' websites showing the winners.

WHAT MORE COULD HAVE BEEN DONE

This event could have been further capitalised on by putting the art entries on to a special web page on both the college's and the accountancy firm's website with an online vote. An e-shot could have been sent to all clients and targets encouraging them to click through and view the images and vote for their favourite. A special award could have been created for the image with the highest number of online votes. In addition, if the accountancy firm had its own blog, it could have written lively and informative articles about how the competition was progressing, culminating with the award ceremony and photographs from the event.

As I mentioned previously, your sponsorship does not necessarily have to be big, or even national or international; small local sponsorship can work equally effectively. Just be sure about your objectives from the outset. Consider whether the sponsorship will reach your target audience. Think creatively around the sponsorship deal; what more can you generate from it?

Q EXAMPLE

I was involved in the sponsorship of an all-female crew in a round-the-world yacht race. In order to capitalise on this, my organisation's logo was on the side of the yacht and a special sail was made with the organisation's name and logo on it. A drinks reception was held onboard the yacht before the crew set sail to which customers and potential customers and the media were invited. This event was covered on local television and in the trade and regional press. A world map was displayed in the office and the staff were able to follow the crew's progress as they competed with other crews. There was even a competition to guess their arrival time and their position at each stage of the race. Press coverage and media interviews in each of the countries the crew sailed into were generated; and as the organisation was international, it benefited from the sponsorship across the world. When the crew reached their home port, a welcome home event at a nearby yacht club was organised, with exclusive tours of the yacht. Customers and potential customers were again invited. There was a photo call, with national media attending, and this generated considerable PR for the organisation.

TOP TIPS

Don't wait for sponsors to approach you. Once you have decided your objective and your target audience, look at how they can be reached by teaming up with other organisations.

Also consider the benefits of working alongside a charity. By doing so you can benefit not only the charity but also make a statement about your company, demonstrating that you have a caring attitude which can be communicated both internally and externally.

ACTION POINT

- Examine your target audience: is sponsorship something that would work well for your organisation? Say whether you think a local, regional or national sponsorship might be best.
- Now brainstorm with your staff regarding the types of organisation you could team up with.
- Looking at them, brainstorm some further ideas of what type of sponsorship might work.
- List all the marketing ideas and activity you might be able to conduct around the sponsorship.
- Refine these ideas and identify local, regional or national organisations you'd like to team up with.
- Write an outline of what you are proposing.
- Get contact details of the relevant organisations. The marketing manager or director might be your first port of call. Arrange a meeting to discuss your ideas.
- If the organisation you are approaching isn't interested then perhaps that is their loss; move on and try another. Keep looking for others; you might find some ideas through reading the local and national press. Or after reading the section below where you can couple sponsorship with sales promotion.

SALES PROMOTION

Sales promotion as a marketing tool is a short-term activity, rather than a long-term strategy. It is designed to boost sales of a certain product, brand or service.

Sales promotion campaigns have many objectives. They:
• Attract customers to your premises
• Heighten consumer awareness
• Encourage repeat sales
• Increase the penetration of new products
• Boost volume sales.

Sales promotion activity can also be carried out in conjunction with other parties in the form of sponsorship. For example, collecting tokens from a product packet (manufacturer), in a certain chain of supermarkets (retailer), to help buy computers for schools (charity/sponsorship). Charity promotions can have enormous PR impact, and can substantially increase brand awareness – but be careful that you match the correct brand with the correct charity.

Types of sales promotion

Tokens
Collecting tokens to be redeemed against a future purchase or to go towards a charity or good cause as previously illustrated with our school example. Another example is where a coffee shop customer has a card, and every time he purchases a cup of coffee, his card is stamped. After so many purchases the customer is then entitled to a free cup of coffee.

Money-off coupons
These tend to be very effective in introducing new and improved products. They can reward loyal users and help improve brand loyalty. They can provide an incentive without having to change the price on the packaging.

Competitions

These can be organised fairly quickly and are relatively easy to manage. They also translate well onto a website. They can secure repeat purchases; but unless the value of your prize is high, the take-up might be slow.

Free samples

This can be expensive and more difficult to administer. If sampling door to door, you will need to organise an outside agency to do this for you. Special packs can be expensive.

Other promotions can include:

- Buy one get one free
- 25% discount
- Buy three for two
- 10% extra
- Give aways in magazines/newspapers/radio campaigns
- Cut out coupons – children go free, two meals for the price of one etc
- Personality endorsements
- Point-of-sale material.

As with all your marketing, you must evaluate the success of it. You need to know from the outset what you wish to achieve. You might wish to measure the number of promotional units taken up or sold, number of new users, or attitudes towards the product from both actual users and potential users.

> Sales promotion should not be viewed in isolation but should work alongside your other marketing activities.

Mobile marketing and sales promotion

Mobile coupons are a fast-growing area. This is where discount coupons are sent to a mobile phone rather than being displayed in a newspaper or magazine or being used as a door drop. It is estimated that over 200 million consumers worldwide will be using mobile coupons by 2013 (Juniper Research). In test pilots, mobile coupons have shown a higher redemption rate than the paper version and are deemed an ideal vehicle for restaurants, entertainment companies, retailers and grocery companies.

Q EXAMPLE

A travel company aimed at students decided to include a mobile marketing element in its campaigns, given that a high proportion of its target market use mobile communications. In its poster advertising and direct marketing literature it added SMS keywords and shortcodes, so that students could simply text to receive a digital or printed brochure at the same time as entering a competition to win an all-expenses-paid trip to Australia.

 ACTION POINT

Examine your range of products or services.

- Where are they on the product lifecycle?
- Can you adopt any sales promotions techniques around them?
- If so, what kind and how much will this cost you?
- Is there a better time of year to adopt a sales promotion technique, eg restaurants and pubs usually offer two-for-the-price-of-one meals, or discounts, to customers in January when trade is slack after the Christmas period.
- You might wish to time your promotion around a special day, such as Valentine's Day.

Decide what is relevant for your organisation. What do you hope to achieve though the promotion?

QUICK RECAP

- *Sponsoring an event, a person, or working with a charity can be an effective way of communicating your message to your target group of customers, and can give you exposure to new groups of potential customers.*
- *Care needs to be taken when choosing who or what to sponsor, as you do not wish to run the risk of portraying a negative image.*
- *Decide first what you hope to achieve through sponsorship.*
- *How much will you have to pay for the sponsorship and what does this cover?*
- *How long will the sponsorship last?*
- *Sales promotion is a short-term activity designed to boost sales of a certain product, brand or service.*

CHAPTER 16

Building a media profile

Editorial coverage is an extremely cost effective and powerful way of raising your organisation's profile and stimulating enquiries. It is said to carry two and a half times the weight of advertising. But the days when reporters were roving the streets in search of a good news story are long gone; it is up to you to supply the media with the news. You do this by sending in your news stories on a regular basis to the media that is relevant to your market and your organisation. In this chapter I examine how you can do this.

WHAT ARE THE BENEFITS?

There are many benefits to building a positive media profile for your organisation.

It can:

• Raise your organisation's visibility and credibility with customers and prospective customers
• Stimulate sales of goods and services
• Set you apart from the competition
• Help to motivate employees – everyone likes to work for a successful organisation
• Help to attract good-quality recruits
• Help to reinforce the other sales and marketing messages you are sending out.

> The secret to successful media coverage is pitching the right story to the right media at the right time to convey the right message to your target audience.

EDITORIAL COVERAGE VS. ADVERTISING

Editorial coverage is not the same as advertising. Advertising is where you have paid for space and therefore can say what you like in that space, as long as it conforms to advertising guidelines. You have control over what you say, whereas editorial space is 'free', so you do not have the same control over what is said. The first lesson therefore to be learned is that it is up to the media owner, or editor, to decide whether he wishes to use your 'story'. Just because you send them something, it doesn't mean to say they will use it. Telephoning the journalist and sounding off is not a good idea. It will only alienate him and guarantee no future coverage. If your story doesn't get used, there could be several reasons for this:

• It has been squeezed out by something else

- You got the timing wrong and missed the deadline
- You failed to explain the significance of your mega breakthrough to the journalist
- Your press announcement was boring
- It was due to plain editorial incompetence!

Perseverance is the key. If your story doesn't get used then move on to the next story and keep a regular flow of good news stories going to the journalist. This will help you to build a good relationship with the media.

The second point is that your news story will get altered and shortened, and the angle might even be changed to one you didn't expect. Journalists do sometimes get names and figures wrong and occasionally misinterpret what you are saying either by accident or, dare I say it, by design. But there are ways of writing your news release that will minimise any errors or misinterpretations by the journalist, which I cover later.

WHAT ARE POSSIBLE NEWS STORIES?

There are many 'news' stories to tell within an organisation. Here are some examples:
- Winning new orders/contracts
- Retirements
- New appointments
- Promotions
- New products or services
- Celebrations, like anniversaries
- Winning awards
- Success of employees
- Involvement in local charities
- Good financial results
- Sales promotions
- Sponsorships
- Celebrity visits and endorsements

- New literature/free information
- Human interest stories – personal achievements.

✎ ACTION POINT

- Scan the local and national newspapers to see what makes the news.
- Look at your trade or professional magazines to see who is hitting the headlines and with what kind of story.
- Develop a journalistic eye and look for the angle, ie the element that makes the story appealing and different.
- Set yourself targets for writing and distributing at least one press release a month.

A WORD ABOUT ANGLES

You can greatly enhance your news story by strengthening or having an angle. Here are some suggestions for angles.

Urgency
- New
- Launched today
- Re-launched
- Improved

Uniqueness
- Believed to be the first
- Unique product
- Unique survey
- The first of its kind

Milestones
- The first customer
- The 100th customer
- The 1,000th customer

Conflict
- Challenges the report
- Challenges the government
- Warns businesses
- Warns the public

Special days
- Valentine's Day
- Mother's Day
- Bonfire Night, 5 November
- Other anniversaries

Others
Your product is:
- The oldest
- The youngest
- The largest
- The smallest
- The biggest
- Unusual
- Bucking the trend

WHERE CAN YOU SEND YOUR STORY?

There are many different types of media. Here are some of them.

National newspapers
- Daily newspapers
- Sunday newspapers

Local newspapers
- Daily local newspapers
- Weekly local newspapers
- Bi-weekly local newspapers

Freesheets
- Community newspapers
- Commuter newspapers

Specialist magazines
- Professional and trade press

Consumer magazines

Radio
- Local
- National

Television
- Local
- National, including cable and satellite channels

Internet sites
- News sites
- Special interest sites
- Blogs
- E-zines
- Social network sites
- Community websites
- Digital radio stations

> You need to ensure that you send your news story to the most relevant media for your market.

You will therefore need to research the relevant media. You can do this by conducting a search on the internet and then clicking through to the publication, programme and/or website. You can also find media directories online where you can conduct an alphabetical search for any target media.

WRITING THE NEWS STORY

When constructing a 'news release' to tell your news story you need to think in terms of a triangle or pyramid in that the whole story, including the angle, is contained in the first paragraph and then fleshed out in subsequent paragraphs.

Headline – what the story is about

The headline is there to catch the journalist's eye and tell him what the story is about. Your headline will rarely be used by the newspaper or magazine. The journalist, editor or subeditor will put their own title to the story, which best fits the style of their publication. Your headline might only be used if you are writing an article to commission, or if you have paid to see the article printed. In the latter case we are not talking about editorial but advertising or advertorial.

Example headline

New Marketing Book Shows Businesses How To Win More Customers In Tough Markets

The first paragraph

The first paragraph is the key to the release. It must contain the whole story, the angle and your organisation's name, where you are based and what you do.

Example first paragraph

A new book, *Successful Marketing*, written by Pauline Rowson and published by Crimson Publishing, aims to live up to its title by showing businesses how to win more customers and increase their sales in a tough economic climate, without spending a fortune.

The second paragraph

The second paragraph provides the details already summarised in paragraph one; the facts and figures if necessary. You might only need one paragraph of explanation, otherwise two will probably be sufficient.

> Example second paragraph
>
> The 200-page book takes readers through a step-by-step approach to drawing up a successful marketing plan. It covers areas such as identifying target customers, how to reach new markets, and how to make advertising and promotion more effective. It also contains sections on viral marketing, website marketing and search engine optimisation and how to conduct e-campaigns.

The third and fourth paragraphs

The third paragraph is a quote and the fourth paragraph might contain more practical facts. Eg if the release is about a new publication or event it can give a contact name and telephone number.

> Example third and fourth paragraphs
>
> Pauline Rowson says, 'This book differs from many on the market because it is practical and straightforward, with lots of exercises and tips for business owners, managers and directors. They will be able to use it as a daily guide as well as helping them to draw up marketing plans that actually work.'
>
> *Successful Marketing* is available online and at all good bookshops. It retails for £9.99.

At the end of the news release put **ENDS,** and the date. Then, **'For further information contact...'** and give details of contacts within your company for the journalist or editor.

So, here is the complete press release:

NEWS RELEASE

New Marketing Book Shows Businesses How To Win More Customers In Tough Markets

A new book, *Successful Marketing*, written by Pauline Rowson and published by Crimson Publishing, aims to live up to its title by showing businesses how to win more customers and increase their sales in a tough economic climate, without spending a fortune.

The 224-page book takes readers through a step-by-step approach to drawing up a successful marketing plan. It covers areas such as identifying target customers, how to reach new markets, and how to make advertising and promotion more effective. It also contains sections on viral marketing, website marketing and search engine optimisation and how to conduct e-campaigns.

Pauline Rowson says, 'This book differs from many on the market because it is practical and straightforward, with lots of exercises and tips for business owners, managers and directors. They will be able to use it as a daily guide as well as helping them to draw up marketing plans that actually work.'

Successful Marketing is available online and at all good bookshops. It retails for £9.99.

For further information contact:
Crimson Publishing
Telephone: 020 8334 1600
Email: info@crimsonpublishing.co.uk
www.crimsonpublishing.co.uk

The following diagram illustrates how the news release is written.

Headline

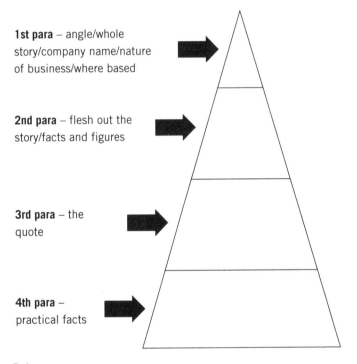

1st para – angle/whole story/company name/nature of business/where based

2nd para – flesh out the story/facts and figures

3rd para – the quote

4th para – practical facts

Ends
Month/year

For further information contact:
Name, company, location, telephone
Email address and website

TOP TIPS

Writing your news release

■ Write **'News Release'** at the top of the document, even if you are going to email it to the journalist or editor.

■ Put 'News Release' – and the headline of your news release in the subject heading of your email.

■ Type your news story neatly with 1.5 paragraph line spacing.

■ Don't underline anything and don't use too many italics or bold.

■ Keep it clean and uncluttered.

■ If printing out your news release to post, only type on one side of paper.

■ Put 'more follows' on the bottom of the page if you are going on to a second page.

■ Don't split a sentence between one page and the next.

■ Staple the pages together.

■ Proofread the release for mistakes before it goes out.

■ Copy your news release into the email message.

■ Send any photographs as attachments, but if it is a strong 'photo story' (see below) you could also insert the photograph in the email message itself with the news release.

■ Email it or send it first-class post.

■ Wherever possible address it to the journalist by name.

■ Alternatively, copy your news release into the contact form on the media's website and send it this way.

EMBARGOES

Embargoes are normally used when a new product or service is about to be launched, or the information contained in the press release is time sensitive and not to be used before a certain date. The media will honour an embargo, and it is certainly useful for them from a planning point of view to have information about the story, or product, before its official release. The release can then appear in the newspaper or magazine, or on the television or radio, on the day the product is launched.

It is usually common practice to write at the top of your release: **Embargo – not to be used before midday on (the date)**

Do not use embargoes unnecessarily as this will only irritate the journalist.

PHOTO STORIES

Some news stories will require a photograph. This is called a photo story. So, what makes a good photo story?

The photo stories are those that are primarily **human interest** stories. For example:

- New staff appointments
- Promotions
- Retirements
- Award winners
- Charity events
- Sponsorship

You can also send photographs with your news releases on:

- The company moving into new premises
- A reception with celebrity guest
- Seminars/conferences
- Mergers/acquisitions/buy outs and buy ins.

To increase your chances of getting your photograph published, it needs to be interesting and creative.

> You need to set the scene. Every picture should tell a story.

Look at the story your release is telling: does the photograph reflect this?

Using a professional photographer

Wherever possible, enlist the services of a professional photographer. This can help you to get your story covered in the media and it will still be cheaper than advertising, and carry more weight.

Some newspapers and magazines will send a press photographer if they think the story warrants it, but this is less frequent these days, and you can't always rely on this happening.

TOP TIPS

If a press photographer does come to photograph you or your staff then here's some of words of advice:

- Visit the other exhibitors and try to do some Do not be bullied or cajoled into shots that you would not like to see in print.
- Visit the other exhibitors and try to do some Don't get into any pose that makes you uncomfortable.

When engaging a professional photographer, make sure that you brief him thoroughly beforehand, as he may need to bring along additional equipment. Ensure you are available when he arrives. If you keep the photographer waiting you can't blame him for charging you for that time! You will need your photographs as digital images so that they can be emailed to the media and added to your website or blog.

A professional photographer will try to put people at their ease. Most people hate being photographed; it is an ordeal that many want over and done with as quickly as possible. This means you also need a friendly photographer and one who works quickly. Nobody wants to be standing around forever. This is not a wedding and there is work to be getting on with.

SUCCESSFUL MARKETING

You will need contact sheets of the shots the photographer has taken preferably the same day as the photo shoot or the following one. These contain a selection of the photographs taken and you can then choose the best shots for your news story.

Doing it yourself
If you decide to take the photograph yourself then ensure that you take tight (close-up) shots of people. Also ensure they are high-quality digital shots.

RULES FOR GOOD MEDIA RELATIONS

Understand the media
Editors and producers have a job to do, and that job is to produce newspapers, magazines or programmes that people want to read or listen to. Your task is to provide them with stories that are suitable for their medium.

Be accessible
The media work to tight deadlines so take calls, or return them, quickly. Failure to respond may mean missed coverage for your organisation.

Don't ask to see copy in advance
Journalists don't like showing you their copy in advance, as experience has shown them that some people can't resist dabbling with the style or changing their minds about what they said.

TOP TIPS
Ask the journalist what his deadline is and ensure you call back within that timescale.

Talk in a 'sound bite'
When you are asked for a comment, make it a 'sound bite'. Use conversational English, not management speak. However, if a journalist telephones you for a comment about something you haven't seen, or something that is slightly contro-

184

versial, you might need time to think about your response. Tell him you will call back within five minutes and then do so. If you do not return the call then you will miss an opportunity for press coverage; and worse, the journalist will know that he cannot rely on you, so you will lose future coverage.

Identify subjects you won't discuss

Be aware of subjects you do not wish to discuss and do not be drawn into discussing them.

TOP TIPS

- Be open, positive and do not lie, as journalists are very good at detecting lies.
- Do not make unsupported claims and avoid negative comments.
- Do not say anything that you would not wish to see in print.
- Do not be aggressive or combative towards a journalist, even if they are like that to you.
- Stay focused and remain polite.
- Ask the journalist what his news slant is, so that you can provide the most useful information.
- Always have ready a few well-rehearsed statements or key points about your organisation you would like to make. This will help you in leading the interview, rather than just responding to it. This is particularly important in television and radio interviewing.

Maintain a friendly relationship with journalists

If a journalist can rely on you to feed him good stories and provide information then you will increase your chances of winning more media coverage.

Don't hound a journalist for story dates

Nothing is more likely to turn a journalist against you than if you pester him to find out when your story is likely to appear.

Don't try to win coverage by too much entertainment

Journalists know there is no such thing as a free lunch and that you are looking for something in return. You can take them out to lunch to thank them for their cooperation, or to find out if they are interested in any particular news items you might be able to supply. You can also use the meal to explain to them that you are keen to raise your media profile and would like to send them stories that would help them. If you know what they are interested in, hopefully you can supply them with the right stories. Journalists don't mind this at all. Remember they are looking for good stories and you can help save them time and energy by providing these.

QUICK RECAP

- *Media coverage is an extremely effective way of raising your organisation's profile.*
- *The secret to successful media coverage is in pitching the right story to the right media at the right time.*
- *There are many 'news' stories to tell within an organisation. Scan the local and national newspapers to see what makes the news.*
- *Review your trade or professional magazines to see who is hitting the headlines and with what kind of story.*
- *Develop a journalistic eye and look for the angle – the element that makes the story appealing and different.*
- *Keep releases short.*
- *When constructing a news release you need to think of a triangle or pyramid.*

CHAPTER 17

Putting it all together: your marketing plan

Many businesses fail in their marketing because they don't undertake the basic groundwork. You shouldn't even look at the promotional tools you can use to market your business until you have understood who your customers are, what they are buying and why they buy, and you have analysed your products and pricing and your marketplace. You also need to be clear about what you want to achieve through your marketing, ie your objectives, and the strategies to engage to help you achieve them. This chapter examines how you can put all this together in your marketing plan.

**TOP
TIPS**

- Don't leap into using a promotional tool until you have thought it through.
- You will need a mix of different promotional marketing tools to achieve your objectives.
- Choose your promotional tools and use them wisely.
- You need to consistently communicate with your target audience in the way they understand.
- You need to consistently look at the products and services you deliver and ensure these are what your customers want.
- You need to consistently look at your organisation and the marketplace in which it operates.

INTERNAL MARKETING

A word about internal marketing before I look at pulling together the marketing plan. It's no good spending money on external marketing – the promotional tools – to find that once you've brought the customer in, something goes wrong inside the organisation and you lose the sale. If the customer has a bad experience he will tell others about it, and you could therefore lose further custom. On the other hand, personal recommendation is a powerful marketing tool.

'Do good work and more work comes from it.'

Loyal and satisfied customers will recommend you and your products and services to others.

However the news is spread about your organisation and its products and services, whether it is online or through traditional word-of-mouth recommendation or campaigns, make sure the message is a positive one.

Having a reputation for good-quality products and services can help you to build a solid and growing customer base. You can also enhance this by consistently communicating with your customers and prospective customers through using some of the effective marketing techniques discussed in this book.

For those other promotional and marketing techniques that haven't been discussed here, such as telemarketing and selling, which require a high level of personal development skills and special training in sales techniques, you might wish to read our sister publication *Successful Sales*.

If you employ staff, make sure they are working for you, not against you. You want motivated and loyal staff who take a pride in delivering to the customer. The staff, the image, and first impressions are all important. Revisit the marketing-orientated questionnaire in Chapter 1 to regularly check if you can tick yes to all the questions. What do you have to do to keep your customers coming back for more? Do it now and keep doing it.

Finally, I have laid out for you on the following pages a summary of marketing action points. If you answer these action points, you should end up with a marketing plan for your business that, I sincerely hope, will bring you every success.

ACTION POINT 1

- Take a look at your organisation and the services or products it produces; are these what the customer wants?
- Do you tap into your customers' comments about your products or services? Have you asked your customers what they want?
- Start now – telephone a sample of customers or devise a questionnaire to capture their comments after a transaction.
- Gain feedback from your staff if they regularly interface with your customers. Do this exercise regularly and analyse the results.

ACTION POINT 2

- Look at your own customer base and analyse who is buying from you.
  - What sort of people are they? What types of business?
  - Where do they come from?
  - How much do they spend?
  - Which are the most profitable sectors?
- Start capturing this information on a database and analyse it on a regular basis.

ACTION POINT 3

- Draw up a list of features for your business, and for each product or service you provide.
- Ask yourself, 'What does this feature mean to the customer?' Put the benefit to the customer alongside that feature.
- Are these benefits promoted strongly in your marketing literature? If they aren't, rewrite your literature and incorporate the benefits.
- Are the benefits prominent on your website? Have you identified the keywords your customers will use for online searches?

ACTION POINT 4

- Look at the volume of sales generated for each product or service.
- Compare this with previous years' performance; then plot your range of products or services on a lifecycle.
- Which products or services would you say are in the maturity or growth phase? Which are in decline?
- Have you any new products or services being developed or introduced? Should you be looking at this area?
- What are you going to do to start this process, and when are you going to do it?

ACTION POINT 5

- Have you developed a strong brand for your products?
- What does that brand mean to you, to your staff, to your customers? Have you asked them?
  - If you all come up with the same or similar words when talking about your products or services, then you are branding, and successfully.
  - If there is a difference, or people can't say what your products represent, then you are failing.
- Do your customers and target customers know what your brand image is? Do you? State it now. List the characteristics of your products/services.

ACTION POINT 6

- Carry out an image audit on your business. Identify those elements that are giving out a favourable image and those that are giving out an unfavourable image. What are you going to do to turn the unfavourable images into favourable ones?
- Conduct the first impressions checklists and identify areas that need to be put right. Make a list of them and say how and when you are going to put them right.

ACTION POINT 7

- Carry out a staff audit.
  - How satisfied are your staff?
  - Do you motivate and train them?
  - Do they know what your organisation stands for?
- Examine your recruitment policies.
  - Have you identified what sort of staff you require?
  - Do you induct them, inform and involve them?

ACTION POINT 8

- Examine your pricing strategies.
  - Are these the correct ones for your objectives and the marketplace?
  - Do you need to change them?

ACTION POINT 9

- Carry out a strengths and weaknesses analysis. This is concerned with the internal aspects of your business. List them and identify action to correct the weaknesses. How are you going to build on your strengths? Don't forget to examine your website and see if it is designed with your customers in mind and that it is maximised for the search engines.
- Carry out an opportunities and threats analysis. This is concerned with factors outside your control in the external market. Identify any opportunities for your organisation. How are you going to exploit these? Also identify the threats – what can you do to minimise these?
- Identify your competitors:
  - Who are they?
  - What are they selling/providing and how?
  - How can you be better or different to them?
  - How/what do you need to change?

ACTION POINT 10

- Set your objectives for the next year. Make sure these are SMART, ie:
  - Specific
  - Measurable
  - Achievable
  - Realistic
  - Timed.

- Identify the marketing strategies you are going to use to help you achieve your objectives.
  - Market penetration
  - Product/service development
  - Market extension
  - Diversification.

ACTION POINT 11

- For each group of target customers and/or each product or service, say what promotional tools you are going to use over the next year to target them and what results you expect.
- Focus on who your customers are, both actual and potential.
- Identify growth areas.
- State what action and the promotional tools you are going to use to target them.
- State when you are going to do this, who will be responsible for seeing that the marketing is carried out and how much it will cost you.

ACTION POINT 12

- Set your budgets and say when you are going to review your plan.

THE MARKETING PLAN

Below are the headings for your marketing plan.

1. Marketing objectives

State these. They should be:
- Specific
- Measurable
- Attainable

- Realistic
- Timed.

2. Current situation analysis

Give a summary of your:
- Strengths
- Weaknesses
- Opportunities
- Threats.

This section should also include information on your:
- Competitors
- Target markets
- Key products/services
- Staff capabilities
- Image
- Competitive edge.

3. Marketing strategy

Identify the key strategies your company is going to take to meet its objectives.

4. Marketing action

Try to break this down by target market sectors, giving marketing action for each sector as appropriate.

Identify the promotional tools needed to target these market segments. These could include:
- Advertising
- Direct marketing campaigns
- E-marketing campaigns
- Viral marketing
- Mobile marketing
- Internet marketing
- Exhibitions
- Publicity
- Sponsorship

- Sales promotion
- Personal selling
- Telemarketing
- Existing customer relations/cross selling initiatives.

5. Set your budget

Cost the above promotional tools and add your budget into your plan. Identify a budget for the development of any new products/ services.

6. Review

Build in a timetable for reviewing the plan – quarterly would be best – and make sure it happens. Take corrective action if you are not meeting your objectives.

Remember:

Focus – Target – Act – Review – Adapt

Business never stands still. If you do nothing then nothing is exactly what you will get in return. Make sure this doesn't happen to you and your organisation.

Good luck!

CHAPTER 18

Quickstart guide:
summary of key points

CHAPTER 1: WHAT IS SUCCESSFUL MARKETING?

- Marketing is a long-term strategy not a short-term one.
- Marketing is a management philosophy that should run right through your business.
- Marketing means getting to know your customers and thinking like them.
- Marketing is giving your customers what they want, when they want it, how they want it and delivering it in a profitable way.
- Marketing is anticipating what your customers will want in the future and ensuring you deliver this.
- Marketing is about creating your services/products with the customer in mind.
- Marketing is making sure your staff are motivated and all pulling in the same direction.
- Marketing is about consistently delivering your promises and innovating to gain a competitive edge.

CHAPTER 2: KNOW YOUR CUSTOMERS

- Identify who your customers are. Break your customers down into easily identifiable groups with similar characteristics.
- Business customers can be broken down into:
  - Industry type
  - Size
  - Geographical area
- Consumers can be broken down into:
  - Socioeconomic groups
  - Type of house
  - Geographical area
  - Lifestyle
  - Lifecycle
  - Age
  - Gender
  - Ethnic origin.

- Examine what each group of customers buy, how much and when.
- Look at the groups of customers in relation to your marketplace:
  - How large is the group?
  - What geographical area does it cover? Is this easily accessible to you?
  - How profitable is the group of customers?
  - How easy is it to enter or win new business from this group of customers?
- Keep in regular touch with your existing customers; try to up sell and cross sell other products and services to them.
- Find out why customers have stopped buying from you and try to win them back.

CHAPTER 3: KNOW WHAT YOUR CUSTOMERS ARE BUYING AND WHY

- Understanding exactly what your customers are buying will help you send the right message to them.
- When people buy, they ask themselves the question, 'What's in it for me?'
- You need to communicate the benefits of your products or services in your advertising and promotional campaigns.
- The two magic words that turn a feature into a benefit are *which means*.
- People generally buy for two reasons: objective and subjective.
- Individuals will buy some products or services to satisfy the basic **physiological needs**. These are the **objective reasons** why people buy.
- The subjective reasons are personal based and are referred to as the **psychological reasons** involved in buying.
- Know your marketplace and your competitors.

CHAPTER 4: DEVELOPING PRODUCTS AND SERVICES THAT YOUR CUSTOMERS WANT

- Constantly develop new products and services to suit your existing customers, or for new customers.
- Look at providing better, newer, different and more profitable products, or ways of supplying your customers.
- The product lifecycle explores the concept that products go through certain phases: introduction, growth, maturity and decline.
- Most companies have a range of products, each of which may be in a different stage of its lifecycle.
- The stage of your product or service will determine the marketing strategy, investment costs and profitability.
- You can extend the lifecycle and halt decline by **adapting the product**. This means taking an existing product or service and adapting it for an existing market, or for a completely new market.
- If sales are declining, you may decide to withdraw the product.
- Ideas for new products or services can come from: talking and listening to your staff; talking and listening to your customers; from your competitors; published research; and the media.
- Ask yourself if you are providing the right products and services to your customers in the best way.

CHAPTER 5: PRICING

- When you set your prices, they won't stay the same forever.
- Be attuned to the marketplace, the competition and changing consumer attitudes.
- Price can sometimes be taken as an indication of quality.
- People will also make a comparison between the product and its 'perceived value'.
- Pricing can also be linked to the packaging.

- You will consider price changes when launching a new product, to help boost an ailing product and as a loss leader to counter competition.

CHAPTER 6: MARKETING TOOLS TO GAIN A COMPETITIVE EDGE

- There are a number of ways you can build a competitive edge, but the key to doing so and maintaining a competitive edge is **consistency**.
- You can build a competitive edge through: branding, image, price, product or service differentiation, and by having a reputation for excellence.
- Branding is used to define identity and helps people relate to the product.
- People will ask themselves if the brand fits with their lifestyle and identity, whether or not it is value for money.
- Various factors go into making up a brand image. These include the product itself, the packaging, the advertising, the brand name, the price, how and where it is distributed and its availability.
- Choosing a brand name can be tricky. The brand name should never contradict the essential product qualities. It should not have unfortunate connotations. It should be easy to say, easily pronounceable, be catchy and should fit onto the packaging.
- Having a clearly defined image for your business, products or services will greatly enhance your organisation's competitiveness and increase sales.
- Building a good reputation for excellence in your field will ensure you get recommendations and repeat business.
- First impressions can be critical. Make sure they are the right impressions.
- When building a competitive edge your staff are vital. Ensure that everyone is working for the organisation, not against it.

- Building a good reputation for excellence in your field will ensure you get recommendations and repeat business.
- Communication plays a key role in developing your staff to provide the desired corporate image.
- Involve your staff, get their feedback and do this on a continuous basis.
- Develop a personality for your organisation and lead it from the **top**.
- Set standards for how you expect your staff to behave.
- Give your staff the right training, not only for their jobs, but also in people skills.
- Measure and monitor performance of your staff.
- Reward your staff – remember to say 'well done' or 'thank you'.

CHAPTER 7: MARKETING PLANNING: DATABASE, SWOT, MARKETING OBJECTIVES AND STRATEGIES

- A database is a vital marketing and management information tool for driving your business forward.
- It should record existing customers and their transactions and review past customer transactions.
- It can be used to personalise your mailings, newsletters and brochures, and to send out regular e-bulletins and e-newsletters.
- A database will: help to identify prospects and their potential to buy; target key customers and prospects with the right messages; monitor the success or otherwise of your marketing activity; identify areas of improvements; monitor sales and decline of sales of products or services.
- The SWOT analysis should be conducted at least twice yearly.
- Your marketing plan should address the weaknesses identified in your organisation and build on its strengths. It should state how you are going to capitalise on the opportunities and what action you are going to take to overcome any threats to the business.

- Marketing objectives should be specific, measurable, achievable, realistic and timed (SMART).
- Don't set too many objectives, because if you can't fulfil them, you will become de-motivated.
- There are four basic marketing strategies to help you achieve your objectives: market penetration, product/service development, market extension, diversification.

CHAPTER 8: THE MARKETING TOOLS

- There are a number of promotional tools you can use. You have to decide which tools, or which mix of tools, are the most appropriate.
- You will need to consider: what you are hoping to achieve, what your budget is and whether or not it is the most appropriate method for that particular group of customers.
- Before you decide to use any promotional tools you should ask: can demand for this product or service be stimulated by using this promotional tool?
- You can't measure the success of the promotional tool unless you know what it is you wish to achieve in the first instance.
- Always track results.
- You must communicate the benefits of what you are offering, in the language that the target market understands and can relate to.
- You must also communicate your image and/or the brand values if appropriate.
- Be consistent in your approach.

CHAPTER 9: ADVERTISING

Before deciding whether or not to advertise you need to be clear:
- What your objective is
- Who you are targeting

- Whether the chosen form of advertising will reach your target customers
- If customers would respond to it
- How your message can be creatively different.

CHAPTER 10: HOW TO MAKE ADVERTISING AND MAILSHOTS WORK

- In order to be effective, advertising must create a sense of familiarity with the target audience.
- People buy what they know and recognise.
- Advertisements over a period of time raise awareness and build credibility.
- The customer must be aware of the brand or company.
- There must be some *understanding* of what the product is and what it will do for the customer.
- The customer must arrive at the mental *conviction* to buy the product.
- The customer must stir himself into *action.*
- Your advertising message should conform to AIDA:
  A = Attention
  I = Interest
  D = Desire
  A = Action.
- Well-targeted and well-designed mailshots can be an extremely successful form of marketing.

CHAPTER 11: EMAIL MARKETING

- Check the legislation in the country you are targeting before embarking on a campaign.
- If you buy in, or rent a list from a third party, you can only use it if it was obtained by that third party on a clear **prior consent** basis.

- Do not conceal your identity when you contact customers by email.
- Provide a valid contact address for subsequent 'opt outs'.
- The older the list, the less likely the recipient is to respond positively to a marketing message.
- The best lists are ones that you build yourself.
- Keep the data clean; personalise messages.
- Ask your customers how they prefer to be contacted.
- Provide a statement of use when you collect details and put this somewhere visible, so that customers can easily read it.
- When writing email copy, be short and to the point; give him a reason to open the email.
- Use language that communicates directly on a one-to-one basis; don't let it look like spam.
- Lead your customers to your website for further details and benefits.
- Test it.

CHAPTER 12: NEWSLETTERS, E-NEWSLETTERS AND CORPORATE BROCHURES

- Newsletters are a very effective marketing tool:
  - They can keep both your existing customers and target customers informed of new products and services.
  - They help to keep your company name in front of your customers on a regular basis.
  - They build credibility and engender a feeling of trust.
- Be clear about your objectives and know your target audience.
- Remind subscribers to forward your e-newsletter to their contacts or friends.
- Newsletters should contain information of value.
- Draw up a publication timetable and stick to it.
- Include a questionnaire to get customer feedback on your products/services.

- Decide if you need a corporate brochure and how you are going to use it.
- Don't have too many people involved in the design of a corporate brochure, because they will all have different views about what they like.
- Stress the **benefits** and write it in a style your customers will respond to.
- Consider making your brochure available as a download through your website.

CHAPTER 13: WEBSITES, BLOGS AND VIRAL MARKETING

- Identify which unique selling points or benefits you are going to emphasise on your website and webpages; these can help you identify keywords.
- When designing and writing your website, remember your target audience.
- Make your website quick and easy to use, have a clean and logical hierarchy to your site and good page structure.
- Keep important information **above the fold**.
- Use links to take your visitor to further information.
- Use plenty of headings, subheadings and white space, which makes it easier to read.
- Use graphics sparingly as they add to the download time.
- Test your website on various internet browsers and window sizes.
- Consider starting a blog or adding one to your website, and remember to update it frequently: search engines love fresh content.
- Update your website regularly.
- Plan how to build links to other websites to increase your search engine ranking.

CHAPTER 14: EXHIBITIONS

- Why are you exhibiting? Be clear on what you hope to gain from attending.
- Ask yourself if it is the right exhibition for your business.
- How are the organisers promoting the exhibition?
- What will it cost?
- Who is responsible for the design of your stand?
- Have at least two people on the stand for the majority of time.
- Track the results of an exhibition.
- Ruthlessly follow up all contacts made, and keep in touch with them.

CHAPTER 15: SPONSORSHIP AND SALES PROMOTION

- Sponsoring an event, a person, or working with a charity can be an effective way of communicating your message to your target group of customers, and can give you exposure to new groups of potential customers.
- Care needs to be taken when choosing who or what to sponsor, as you do not wish to run the risk of portraying a negative image.
- Decide first what you hope to achieve through sponsorship.
- How much will you have to pay for the sponsorship and what does this cover?
- How long will the sponsorship last?
- Sales promotion is a short-term activity designed to boost sales of a certain product, brand or service.

CHAPTER 16: BUILDING A MEDIA PROFILE

- Media coverage is an extremely effective way of raising your organisation's profile.
- The secret to successful media coverage is in pitching the right story to the right media at the right time.
- There are many 'news' stories to tell within an organisation. Scan the local and national newspapers to see what makes the news.
- Review your trade or professional magazines to see who is hitting the headlines and with what kind of story.
- Develop a journalistic eye and look for the angle – the element that makes the story appealing and different.
- Keep releases short.
- When constructing a news release, you need to think of a triangle or pyramid.

CHAPTER 19

Troubleshooting

Q: I'm not getting any response to my mailshots, why?

First look at your target list – are you mailing the right people? Have you correctly identified who your target audience is? How up to date is your list? Are you getting many returned to you as 'gone away' or 'not at this address'? It is always a good idea to clean your list before sending out a mailshot, so if you can, telephone the contacts you have and check that the person on your mailing list is still there and that they are the correct contact. If you have purchased a list then it should be up to date, although mailing houses allow for a certain number of returns and this will be reflected in the fee that you pay them for the list.

Next, examine your mailer. Does it conform to AIDA – Attention, Interest, Desire, Action? Is your headline (call to action) strong enough? Have you run it through the headline analyser to see how powerful an attention grabber it is? Are the benefits strong enough? Remember there must be something for the reader wherever he looks in the letter or mailing leaflet/brochure. How powerful is your offer? Can you make it even more powerful?

Finally, have you made it easy for your reader to respond? Give them boxes to tick or a website to refer to for more information.

Responses to mailshots can generally be as low as 2%. You can lift this response by following the above, and by following up the mailer with a telephone call. You can also lift response through continuing with your mailing programme, so that the second, third and fourth mailers will generate greater response.

Q: My press releases aren't getting into the newspapers and magazines, why?

First, is the story strong enough? What might seem like an earth-shattering, exciting story to you might hold no interest for the media. There is a little ditty in the newspaper business used as a test of newsworthiness:

'Dog kills cat is not news (because it can happen)

Boy kills cat merits just one paragraph because boys can be beastly

Girl kills cat is worth two paragraphs because girls are less beastly

Mouse kills cat is front page funny, in bold

Nun eats cat is a page 3 lead

FERGIE fries cat is a splash – but only in a bad week.'

Fred Plester, *Bedfordshire on Sunday*

So examine your press story and ask yourself if the readers of the newspaper or magazine, or the listeners to the radio programme you have targeted your news story at, would be really interested in it.

Whilst the news story might be strong, you might have failed to convey this because your angle isn't powerful enough or you have buried the most important aspect of your news release in the final paragraph. The angle and the whole story must be encapsulated in the first paragraph. When writing the news release, think of a triangle. Start with the main story and angle in the first paragraph and then expand on it. It is more like writing a summary than an essay.

Have you got your timing right? Perhaps you sent the release out too late. Also look at who you sent the release to – is it the correct medium for that story? Have you sent it to the correct journalist or editor?

If you have complied with all this and you still don't get coverage, then don't give up. It can take time to build relationships with journalists. Keep going and keep improving your news releases.

Q: We're losing sales on a couple of product lines. What should we do?

Ask yourself why are you losing sales? Have the products been on sale for a long time and have they reached maturity? Has demand for these products been overtaken by something new from a competitor, or has consumer taste or technology left them looking outdated?

Perhaps the customer base you were selling them to has aged and is declining, and the products don't appeal to a younger generation. In essence, examine your marketplace and your customer base for these products and see what has changed to make them less attractive than they once were.

Then ask yourself if you could re-launch these products, or one of them, after redesigning or enhancing them. How much would that cost? Would you be able to get a return on that investment by attracting a new group of customers and stimulating sales? Or perhaps you could keep the products as they are but look for a new market in which to sell them, going abroad for example, or further afield into a new geographical area.

It may be that the product has had its day and no amount of investment in re-launching it would be worthwhile. If this is so you can either ditch it or perhaps sell off stock at a special offer or put it in a promotion.

Q: How can I boost response to my email campaigns?

Make sure that the people you are targeting with your e-shots or e-newsletters are the correct audience. What do you know about them? What kind of style of e-shot would appeal to them? What kind of content? Should it be fun and wacky, or more sober? Think about your audience and your products/services and deliver content to them that would appeal to them.

As with mailshots you need to ensure that the copy is strong enough to generate interest, build desire and stimulate action. Is your subject header strong enough to compel people to open the email and then read it? Check it out with the headline analyser to see how persuasive it is. Does the content of the e-shot appeal to the reader personally or does it look like spam and will therefore be quickly deleted?

Is it easy for your reader to click through and read more information on your website? Perhaps you can put a strong special online offer in your e-shot that will compel people to 'read more' on the website.

Q: My advertisements aren't generating any replies, why?

Firstly, examine where you have advertised, then ask yourself if it is the correct medium for your target audience. If your target audience doesn't read that publication or listen to that radio station, or use those internet sites where you have advertised, then obviously you will not get the desired response and you will have wasted money.

Secondly, look at how the message is treated in your advertisement. Does it communicate to the target audience in the way that they would identify with and respond to? It's no good having a beautifully designed or executed advertisement that could win awards if it is sending out the wrong message to your target audience.

How strong is the message in terms of AIDA – has the advertisement been designed to grab the attention? Are there strong benefits in the copy which will persuade people to respond? Have you made it easy for them to respond?

Have you taken a one-off advertisement or booked a series? One-off advertisements generally have little effect. People buy what they are familiar with, so you need to reinforce the advertising message either by repeating it or combining it with other marketing tools, such as media coverage, or a mailing or emailing campaign.

Q: I haven't got a lot of money to spend on marketing so where is the best place to spend it?

The key factor in making your marketing work, and therefore the money you spend work, is ensuring you are marketing to the correct target audience. It's not a bit of good having a wonderful mailing or advertising campaign if it is aimed at the wrong people. So make sure you undertake the basic ground work before you spend any money, ie you will need to be able to answer the fundamental questions:

- Who are my customers?
- What do I know about them?
- What do they want?
- What do they buy and why do they buy it?
- How can I reach them?

Once you have the answers to these questions you can ask: what would they respond to? This will then tell you where to concentrate your marketing efforts.

When examining your target markets, you might also look at which groups of customers are easy to reach and require fairly simple marketing approaches such as a regular telephone call along with an email campaign, and which are harder to reach and convert but could be lucrative markets. These will need perhaps a more active marketing campaign over a longer period of time. As with all your marketing, the key to being successful is consistency.

Q: Should I engage a marketing or advertising agency to help me? If so, how much would I be looking at spending and what should I expect from them?

If you feel you don't have the time or expertise to develop and execute successful marketing campaigns, then there are many marketing agencies and consultancies that can help you.

Firstly, decide what kind of help you require and therefore what type of agency or expert to engage.

Advertising agencies will handle advertising campaigns for you, which will probably include mailing and emailing campaigns; they can also advise on web design, newsletters and e-newsletters.

A PR agency will handle your media relations for you, come up with ideas for news stories, and write and submit news releases to the media. PR agencies can also provide media training and help with writing content for newsletters and e-newsletters.

Design agencies will design advertisements, brochures, newsletters, websites and other marketing material, but might not be best placed to give you in-depth marketing, PR and advertising advice.

Or you might wish to engage what is called 'a full-service marketing agency' which can provide all of the above, either directly or by working in partnership with specialists they trust and whose expertise they endorse.

Secondly, before engaging anyone, you should ask them the following questions:

- What knowledge do you have of my business sector and my business?
- What experience does your team have?
- Who will work on my account and be my main point of contact?
- What services do you provide?
- What is the mix of your client portfolio?
- What are your terms of business and how do you charge?

Also ask to see case studies/campaigns/testimonials to verify track records and for the names of some of their existing clients so that you can contact them for references.

When measuring the performance of an agency, look at their ability to deliver what they have promised and whether or not they have been able to meet the deadlines agreed. Personal relationships are important, so you must be able to get on with the agency staff.

Here's a checklist to help you when selecting an agency:
1. Define your requirements
2. Research for a suitable agency
3. Draw up a list of possibles
4. Invite a credentials pitch
5. Draw up a shortlist of probables – approximately two or three
6. Invite formal presentations
7. Decide
8. Sign contract
   – What is expected of both parties?
   – Terms of payment/how payment is made
9. Review on regular basis

Most consultancies/agencies charge on an hourly rate basis for their time and expertise. Generally speaking, the bigger the agency, the more expensive. Some will want a retained fee, ie you pay a certain amount each month; others are happy to invoice you at the end of each month on a time spent basis. Whatever is agreed, make sure you fully understand it and are comfortable with what has been agreed before committing yourself. It can be money well spent if you get the results and increased profile and sales you need, and it can save you and your staff valuable time.

Index